Qualified

Mia Love

Qualified

*Finding Your Voice,
Leading with Character,
and Empowering Others*

Mia Love

CENTER
STREET

NASHVILLE • NEW YORK

Center Street
Hachette Book Group
1290 Avenue of the Americas, New York, NY 10104
centerstreet.com
twitter.com/centerstreet

First Edition: January 2023

Center Street is a division of Hachette Book Group, Inc. The Center Street name and logo are trademarks of Hachette Book Group, Inc.

The publisher is not responsible for websites (or their content) that are not owned by the publisher.

The Hachette Speakers Bureau provides a wide range of authors for speaking events. To find out more, go to www.HachetteSpeakersBureau .com or call (866) 376-6591.

Library of Congress Cataloging-in-Publication Data has been applied for.

ISBNs: 978-1-5460-0326-7 (hardcover), 978-1-5460-0328-1 (ebook)

Printed in the United States of America

LSC-C

Printing 1, 2022

This book is dedicated first to my dad and mom, Jean Maxine and Marie Bourdeau. My mother, who didn't even graduate high school, has provided me a lifetime of education, wisdom, and inspiration. My dad made extraordinarily difficult decisions to pursue a better life in a place he had only heard about—America. They both showed me what commitment, sacrifice, and service look like.

My parents made excruciating choices to leave everything they knew in Haiti, to give their children the best opportunities to rise and reach their potential in the land of the free. My parents taught me that the idea of America was worth risking everything for. Once here, they taught me that each of us has a duty and obligation to use our gifts and talents to give back and make a difference.

To my husband, Jason, the love of my life, and our children, Alessa, Abigail, and Peyton: I am humbly thankful as a wife and mother for the great sacrifices each of you have made so that, together, WE could serve our community and country.

A reminder to each of my children: You now have the responsibility, standing on the broad shoulders of those who have gone before you, to teach your children to use their gifts and talents to make your country, your state, and your community a better place. I echo to you what my dad declared to me: "You will give back." Remember that giving back is a joyful duty and the path to true success and happiness as you pursue your version of the American Dream.

Contents

Foreword

I first saw Mia when she spoke at the 2012 Republican National Convention, one of the biggest stages in all of politics. She was hailed as the next up-and-coming political star, a conservative who could speak to women, young people, and communities of color Republicans had struggled to reach. She was a Black Republican nominated for Congress in the largely white state of Utah. I was impressed by her from a distance before having the opportunity to really get to know her. And, as it sometimes happens in life, the private person you get to know is even better than the public one you thought you knew.

I first met Mia in a small committee conference room during her freshman orientation in November 2014. I cannot explain how or why we immediately hit it off, but we did. She often joined Senator Tim Scott, Johnny Ratcliffe, and me for dinner, where I was able to get to know who she was outside of the floor of the house. The "rising star" I saw on national television in the summer of 2012 had no interest in being a star. She was singularly focused on work, constantly seeking to have not only command of the issues but command on how to communicate those issues. Mia's background was not in law nor the courts, but she wanted to be the most effective questioner and communicator she could be during committee hearings, so she worked at it.

What stood out to me about Mia during our time in Congress was her passion for this country. It is a passion that often comes from the children of immigrants, new Americans in love with what this country offers. She had this effervescent hope, the kind of hope that comes from living it. She lived the power of education. She lived what it means to thrive even against most odds. She lived economic empowerment, self-confidence, and a belief that in America, even as a conservative Black woman, you can rise to the heights of a political party.

Mia was targeted for defeat from the moment she first arrived in Congress. It was almost as if Mia was what the other side feared the most. And therefore, she had to work twice as hard to get to Congress and twice as hard to stay there. So in addition to being a mother, a spouse, a member of Congress, highly in demand across the country to speak the message of conservatism, she was constantly trying to fend off national attacks. From the moment she won an election she had to begin the fight for the one to come. It would be exhausting for most of us, but most of us are not made the way Mia is. Always that smile.

Her history is inspiring. Her history is something everyone can celebrate regardless of their political beliefs or station in life. But it is not her history that made her one of my closest colleagues; it was and is her present. It was and remains this uncontrollable combination of energy, work ethic, character, and devotion to faith and family. When Tim Scott, John Ratcliffe, and I would see the top of her head climbing the stairs at the restaurant we frequented one of us would invariably say, "Here comes Hurricane Mia." It was a hurricane of hope that brightened our lives, and I am convinced it will brighten yours as well.

If you ever doubt what hard work, a belief in yourself, education, character, and doing the right thing even when others do not, can do and how it can impact everyone you meet, read her story and doubt no more.

—*Trey Gowdy*

Qualified

Introduction

Have you ever felt so unprepared, uncertain, and unqualified that you had a perpetual pit in your stomach? Have you ever had experts and elites constantly saying you were in over your head and so incredibly incompetent that you wondered if it was worth getting out of bed in the morning? Have you ever faced a never-ending feed of social media posts challenging your integrity and intelligence? Have you experienced suffocating stress from a seemingly endless stream of requests, demands, and commitments? Have you endured a daily dose of overwhelming anxiety that you aren't good enough, aren't doing enough, and aren't qualified enough to fulfill any of the roles you play in your life? Welcome to membership in the United States Congress.

If you have ever wondered if you were good enough, smart enough, Black or white enough, conservative or liberal enough—Congress will multiply and intensify those feelings. I had a lot of these "unqualified" and "not enough" challenges, like many of you, before I was elected to Congress. And they were magnified until I finally decided that enough was enough.

If you are like me, you or someone close to you has experienced imposter syndrome and worried that people may find out that you really aren't as good as those glossy pictures look—that your house isn't in perfect order, your kids have challenges, your "put-together" posts on social media hide your messiness, or that your workout selfie may be hiding how exhausted you really are. You are not alone!

Being a member of Congress can compound and exacerbate any and every bit of self-doubt you have ever experienced. The rat-race and chase of Congress keeps you questioning yourself and running 24/7.

Running!

I learned to run on little sleep. I learned to run an office. I got very good at running in heels—only because—well, shoes matter!

Running to meetings. Running late. Running to meet constituents. Running to or from reporters. Running to vote. Running scared. Running out of patience. Running to catch a plane. Running into buzzsaws. Running to town halls. Running out of energy. Running for reelection. Running, running, running!

Running. I love running. At least I thought I did. One of my first campaign videos was centered on my love of running, which led to my running for Congress. I had no idea what kind of running I was getting into. I didn't realize that running in Washington is designed by both Republican and Democratic leadership to control individual members.

Party leaders on both sides of the political aisle are united on one thing—keeping members off-balance, distracted, and dependent on the party to help them win reelection. It is much easier to keep the members of your caucus in line—and voting the way the Democratic or Republican bosses want—if the members believe they are only one step out of line from being defeated in a primary election.

Political party leaders are very good at reminding you that you really don't belong and that you are lucky to be in Congress. They also remind you regularly how much you need them. The media clobbers you for every slip of the tongue or inarticulate moment. Twitter trolls eviscerate everything from your hair and makeup to your comments on a cable news network.

You may even have the person who occupies the highest office in the land come after you for not bowing to his ego or genuflecting to his arrogance and self-importance.

To have a president of the United States of America, who seemed incapable of having relationships—only convenient transactions—mock you after a tough election loss or call your ancestorial home a "shithole" can be devastating, disconcerting, and disappointing. (More on the forty-fifth president in chapter 12.)

All of it is actually enough to make you want to just run away.

I learned to just run instead.

On my first morning in Washington, my husband, Jason, and I went for a run. Of course, we ran on the National Mall. It became a fitting symbol for my service to the people of Utah and the nation.

As Jason and I ran along, I was amazed that everything seemed to be under construction. In fact, I did a social media post talking about how Washington was broken and in desperate need of repair.

I realized on that first run that I was also going to need to engage in continuous improvement and repair. Doubts about whether or not I was truly qualified and up to the job raced through my mind in those early moments and days in DC. Although I didn't doubt my character or my commitment, the noisy chatter and clamor from politicians and pundits was disorienting.

Running had always been my quiet space. Running cleared my mind and enabled me to tap into my true, inner, authentic self. My regular running for exercise and breathing space became the best way to deal with my 24/7 running as a member of Congress.

I am convinced that any run in America's capital city should end at the Lincoln Memorial. Mine often did.

As a Black woman with no formal political education who was standing in a predominantly white male–dominated political field, standing in front of Abraham Lincoln was powerfully ironic and ironically empowering. I often faced moments of anxiety and self-doubt. Somehow, gazing up at the majestic statue reminded me that I had something to offer the nation and the people I represented. I had a story to tell. I had a voice that could make a difference.

But looking at Lincoln wasn't enough. I had to look back across the National Mall toward the Capitol, where my work would be done in "the people's house."

Looking out toward the Capitol often gave me pause. Yet, I knew in that moment that Lincoln had my back. Those who fought to preserve the Union had created space for me to embrace my story, find my voice, *and* help others do the same.

I also had Representative Lee Zeldin. Lee and I met when I was a mayor and he was in the New York State Senate. We both attended the Aspen Rodel Leadership Summit. Knowing that Washington was an "every man and woman for themselves" kind of place, it is often difficult to know whom you can truly trust. Lee and I made a pact that very first day of orientation that we would have each other's back. We would always be a safe place as friends, first and last, in a world of savage politics. Our families became close. Diana—my ride or die, as I referred to her—and I were close. Jason and Lee also became very close. Our safe place, our pact and friendship, remain intact to this very day.

With Lincoln and Lee at my back, I could gain some confidence for what I needed to do on Capitol Hill. I instinctively and deeply understood that America was still working to live up to the principles we often professed to believe in—equality, justice, and opportunity for all. But at least we had a chance to make our union more perfect.

I wanted desperately to do my part. That often led me to bow my head in prayer in order to gather hope, confidence, and strength to do the right thing in the right way to get the right result for "we the people."

When you stand on the steps of the Lincoln Memorial and bow your head, you will see chiseled in one of those stone steps the words "I have a Dream." It is on that spot in August 1963 that Dr. Martin Luther King Jr. offered one of the greatest speeches ever delivered.

His words still echo down the National Mall, across the nation, and around the world. "I have a dream that my four little children will one day live in a nation where they will not be judged by the color of their skin but by the content of their character."[1]

Dr. King had a dream. I had a dream. Dr. King's words contained the answer to all my feelings of being uncertain, unprepared, and unqualified.

I was qualified because of the content of my character.

Taking a journey of self-discovery was required both to fully understand the content of my character and galvanize those parts of my character that were vital to my success. Yes, there were parts of my journey where I discovered things I didn't like, things I needed to change, and areas in which I needed to improve.

I was qualified because character had been instilled in me from my parents who ran, fought, and sacrificed their way out of an impoverished and devastatingly corrupt nation in pursuit of an improbable dream.

It turns out that running for freedom was in my genes. It was part of my story, part of my history, and part of the content of my character.

My father knew what it meant to run for freedom—because he had. It began in 1958 in Haiti during a night of running and finding refuge in a sewage pipe.

My father, Jean Maxine Bourdeau, was just fourteen years old when he ran from a gun-wielding member of the Tonton Macoute—the thugs representing the paramilitary dictator leader in Haiti. The only path of safety available to him in that terrifying moment was an open sewage pipe. He scurried inside and spent the whole night there.

It was not that sprint in the darkness away from danger or hiding like a terrified animal in that pipe that changed the course of my father's life—and mine. It was what happened the following morning.

My father cautiously made his way home after the danger passed and found his mother in mourning. She knew about the events of the night. At that time in Haiti, if a fourteen-year-old boy didn't come home at night, every mother knew he was dead.

When my father had not returned from town, his mother was certain he had been killed. My father was shocked by his mother's broken spirit. The haunting despair and terror in his mother's eyes changed my dad forever. It sparked and then seared into his soul a passionate desire and need to race for freedom and find opportunity.

I heard this story often while growing up. It is infused into my character. I never cease to be amazed that it really was not his run from death or a night in hiding that changed everything for my dad; the transformation of his character began with the look in his mother's eyes.

A mother's eyes should hold promise and confidence, not panic and uncertainty. In that very moment, my father made a solemn promise to himself that he would not raise his children among the torments his mother had endured. He would find a refuge for his own family in the safest place he could imagine, a place he'd only heard of—the United States of America.

Running toward freedom. Racing toward the dream of America. Dad had his doubts about whether he was qualified, capable, and willing to run down an incredibly uncertain path. The content of his character and that of his mother pushed him forward—doubts, fears, and all.

The American Dream was a seemingly impossible dream for a kid like my father living in Haiti at the time. But, defeating all odds, Dad married my mother, Marie, who shared the same dream, and together they made a plan.

A good friend, Boyd Matheson, recently shared with me a version of something he has presented on his KSL NewsRadio show *Inside Sources*, in print for the *Deseret News*, and in numerous speeches across the country—something that really struck me:

> Our finest hours as a nation have not come about when things were certain and settled. The most important breakthroughs and break-withs, triumphs and transformations occur within the parentheses of a crazy idea.
>
> Within the parentheses of a crazy idea, the foundation of a new nation, conceived in liberty and committed to the principle that all men are created equal, was laid.

Within the parentheses of a crazy idea, a civil war, and even world wars, were waged, including tide-turning battles at Gettysburg and the beaches of Normandy, to win freedom for millions.

Within the parentheses of a crazy idea, game-changing innovations like light bulbs, steam engines, automobiles, and countless entrepreneurial endeavors have been launched.

Within the parentheses of a crazy idea, Rosa Parks took a seat, Martin Luther King took a stand, and Jackie Robinson broke the barrier on America's long and winding road to live up to its ideals.

Within the parentheses of a crazy idea, the Wright Brothers took a flight that eventually propelled small steps into giant leaps for mankind.

Within the parentheses of a crazy idea, women suffragettes plowed the ground that ultimately provided the right to vote to women.[2]

My parents were prepared to insert their own crazy idea within those open parentheses. Their crazy idea included a plan of significant sacrifice and humbling hardship in their quest for freedom and a future where their children would be judged by the content of their character.

After much scrimping and saving, my parents earned

enough money for the airfare and tourist visas to America—which, as challenging as it was, really was the easy part of their crazy pursuit of a better life.

The hard part?

My father went first. I am sure that was beyond difficult for my mother, my brother, and my sister. My mother had to answer the cries of those two little ones: "Where is Daddy?" and "When will Daddy come back?" Such questions, I am sure, pained my mother. How do you explain such separation and sacrifice to a child? This period of separation was simply a prelude to harder, more difficult days ahead.

Finally, it was time for my mother to join him. It would require her to leave those two young children behind with family in Haiti and travel to the United States.

In a moment still incomprehensible to me, my mother made a gut-wrenching decision and stepped into the unknown. As my mother was getting ready to depart, my brother begged her not to get on that "white bird" that took Daddy away. In his little-boy mind, Daddy had not returned, and the frightening idea of his mother leaving too must have broken his tender heart.

With both of her young children screaming and wailing in tears, my mother had to step onto the plane.

This was no small step; it was a giant leap of cosmic proportions. My heart still aches for my mother when I think of that scene.

In total, my parents spent five years apart from their two eldest children. I cannot imagine how that must have felt: the doubts they must have had, the uncertainty that must have accompanied so many distressing moments, and even the shame that they probably felt from the judging eyes of those who questioned why parents would leave their children behind. I am sure they wondered if they had done the right thing, if their children were being taken care of. I know they shed many tears while longing to be reunited.

Through it all, my parents kept their faith in the content of their character, their prospects in the new community they had found in America, and the hope of good days to come. My parents finally secured their American citizenship, thereby establishing a secure foothold on their dream of a brighter future. It was during this time that I was born in Brooklyn, New York.

Interestingly, I didn't meet my older brother and sister until I was five years old. That was a little confusing for me, having spent five years as an only child. After bringing their eldest children to the United States, my parents finally had their family together, and a future filled with promise was ahead.

The road to citizenship for my parents was improbable and sometimes excruciating. Within the parentheses of their crazy idea, they took each step mindful of the infinite possibilities in their children's future as

Americans. Character was being forged and qualified; contributing citizens were being raised.

We were taught to appreciate the freedoms—and the heavy responsibilities—of living in this country. We were raised to love the United States of America. We were conscious of the miracle of clean water, a well-stocked grocery store, orderly elections, a limited government with checks and balances, and an ethical police and military that would not chase children into hiding. It was pounded deep into the foundation of our minds that we would not be takers; we would give back.

Character counted in my home. It would be by the content of our character that we would be judged. Character is forged over time. I believe that we are all products of our past experiences. It's the layers upon layers of our actions, the decisions we've made, and the decisions made for us by our ancestors that make up our life and shape our story.

The stories, dreams, and heroic experiences we are told of as we're growing up are stored as images and powerful memories in our minds. Down through the ages, the events and experiences of those who came before us were born to mothers and fathers and transferred to them by their mother's mothers and father's fathers long ago. Such stories, traditions, values, and beliefs have a direct impact on where we begin our individual journeys and what we believe is true.

What we believe about ourselves influences the decisions we make, the opportunities we take, and the ones we don't. If you don't believe you can, you won't do it. If you believe you are unworthy or unqualified, you won't respond when the opportunity of a lifetime is presented to you. The building of character is a cottage industry.

In the chapters that follow, I hope you will see yourself and come to know with certainty that you are qualified because of the content of your character. Through my experiences and those of others, I want you to join me on a journey of discovery that will help you overcome doubt, believe in yourself, and see the possibilities the future holds for you.

The race toward evaluating and strengthening the content of your character is not easy. But like a great morning run on the National Mall, I promise it will be worth it.

Part of the reason for why I'm writing is for the content of my children's character. I want to pass on the lessons learned—the knowledge, principles, and deep history of our family.

This book is for my minority friends who want to know why I stand for the principles I passionately profess.

This book is for women who struggle with anxiety and self-doubt every day despite their ample qualifications. Women are still unconfident applying for the jobs they are fully capable of pursuing. Women apply for a job only if they meet 100 percent of the qualifications, while men apply based on meeting only 60 percent, according to a Hewlett Packard internal report.[3]

Similarly, it is easy to see that there is an obvious lack of representation of minority groups in our nation's largest area of influence and power—positions in government. Rather than standing in a place of weakness, being convinced by others that you are a victim or that you don't belong, I want you to feel empowered and confident. In the place where the most good could be done to shift, change, and improve lives, far too many minorities are standing on the sidelines rather than confidently getting into the field.

This book is for you and your children. I sincerely hope that our journey together will provide you with a message of encouragement and a plan for personal empowerment.

You have a story—own it. You have a voice—raise it. Then lead and help others do the same. You are qualified by the content of your character.

CHAPTER 1

Do I Belong in a Sea of Old White Men?

As I stood in the wings of the stage at the 2012 Republican National Convention, I took it all in. There were so many people, so many white faces, so many cowboy hats. The thought crossed my mind that I was bringing color to a sea of mostly old white men. Echoes from *Sesame Street* easily flowed to my mind: "One of these things is not like the others."[1]

I was clearly not the same.

I was about to step onto the national stage as a Black, female, mayor, mother, and wife. A first-generation American—a unicorn at the time in the Republican Party.

My nervousness at that moment had me questioning my qualifications and wondering if I truly belonged on such a massive stage, in such an enormous arena, with such high stakes for the Republican Party.

The national GOP leadership for the nominating convention had positioned me as a rising star, announcing me as a voice worth hearing. I did not feel qualified in that moment.

Boyd Matheson, my speechwriter at the time, sensed my rising worry backstage and reminded me of who I was and why I was qualified and ready for the opportunity of a lifetime.

During our preparation for the speech, Boyd had shared an account of what Neil Armstrong was purported to have mumbled after his famous "One small step for man, one giant leap for mankind" moment: "Just like drill." The moment was exactly what Armstrong and thousands of members of the NASA space team had practiced, planned, and prepared for. Whether apocryphal or actually uttered, the message was the same for both an Apollo astronaut and an out-of-her-element political newbie.

Those three simple words, "just like drill," had become my mantra when I was faced with uncertainty and questioned my qualifications. Boyd reminded me that heroic moments were years in the making. Dull practice, hard choices, delayed gratification, quiet discipline, endless seeking, and digging deep to find my core principles—these are the seeds of qualified confidence that eventually lead to historic harvests.

More than a decade earlier, I'd felt the call to be a voice for my neighbors, then I ran for mayor, and now I hoped to take my hard-won local governing lessons to Washington. The journey was filled with personal, interpersonal, and community drills of every kind.

I was thrown a lot of sharp questions about my political leanings and background from politicos, power brokers, and people of color. Pundits could obviously see I was "not like the others" and struggled to put me into a neat and tidy political box. How could I possibly be a Republican when everything about me seemed to not belong in the stereotypical conservative box?

All of that can really make you question your qualifications. I found myself asking, "Do I really belong?"

Panic-filled adrenaline had my mind racing. I was reliving so many moments and memories while recalling vital lessons I had learned along the extraordinary journey that led up to that moment on that big stage.

I remembered that feeling confidently qualified is the result of an arduous and sometimes lonely journey. It usually begins with a significant opportunity being presented to you. That opportunity then causes you to question yourself, your qualifications, and your character. If you lean into the opportunity, it will help you discover the path to owning your story, recognizing your qualifications, and ultimately finding and raising your voice.

The journey is long. The path can be fraught with fear, filled with obstacles, and punctuated with confidence-undermining scrutiny, negativity, and uncertainty. It is the journey of a lifetime, and it begins with crucial questions.

Musicals have been a driving force in my journey from the time I was young. You will see later in this book how the stage helped me find, understand, come to value, and ultimately raise my voice. Stage productions stir me, and the lessons found in the characters regularly lead me to think deeper and think differently about my life, my goals, my roles, and my responsibilities.

In the Broadway classic *Les Misérables*, the hero Jean Valjean poses the ultimate question, "Who am I?" Valjean was arrested after having stolen a loaf of bread and then spent agonizing years in a chain gang. Finally paroled, he finds it difficult to find a way to earn a living as his official papers contain a reference to his criminal past.

Taken in by a humble priest, Valjean is faced with an opportunity to steal valuable candlesticks and begin a new life with enough funds to provide for himself. After stealing the candlesticks, he is caught by the police and brought before the priest for identification. Amazingly, the priest declares that Valjean didn't steal the candlesticks; they were a gift. He even chooses to give him another. The kindly priest sends the authorities away and charges Valjean to go build a life and make a difference. (I can always hear my dad's voice in that charge.)

It is a poignant moment as Valjean reviews who he once was, who he currently seems to be, the power of his oppressor, and what the future holds. Valjean is really questioning who he is at his core. He begins a new journey wondering what he is willing to stand up and speak out for—regardless of the consequences.

Valjean wonders if there is any place, any community, any business, or any relationship, human or divine, where he is qualified to belong.

I know what that feels like.

My mind then drifted back to the Utah State Republican Convention where I had, in a major upset, secured the nomination. I entered the race for the newly created Fourth Congressional District as the longest of long shots. There was a group of men who had had their eyes on the race for years. A number of them were members of the Utah State Legislature and were part of an exclusive club called the Patrick Henry Caucus. Steve Sandstrom and Carl Wimmer, in particular, had worked with the delegates for a very long time. They had the Patrick Henry Caucus supporting them. And they had worked really hard with the delegates.

In 2010, three-term incumbent Utah Republican

senator Bob Bennett was running for reelection. But all these Patrick Henry Caucus members had worked to get delegates elected to the convention who were much more conservative and definitely antiestablishment than Bennett was. All of these people I was running against had worked on the campaign that ultimately elected Republican Mike Lee to the Senate.

So my opponents had worked with these delegates for two years, knew them well, and worked with most of them directly. It seemed that they all belonged, and I clearly didn't.

Then all of a sudden, I had support from congressional leaders in Washington. I had the support of Paul Ryan, Kevin McCarthy, and Eric Cantor. While that was amazing to me, it further put me on the outside—on the she-doesn't-belong train.

Interestingly, the support I got from Paul Ryan actually began with his wife, Janna. She had seen an online video that The Church of Jesus Christ of Latter-day Saints had done on my story. Janna Ryan put that video right in front of Paul and said, "You need to help her."

At the beginning, it didn't seem like it would help in the hyper-antiestablishment state convention. I will return to this later, and how it proved providential.

On the day of the state convention, things were really intense. At that time in Utah, the state GOP convention delegates could determine whether or not there was a primary or whether a candidate would be the nominee and go straight to the November general election ballot. To avoid a primary, you had to get more than 60 percent of the delegate vote. I was hoping to keep any of the other candidates from getting to 60 percent and squeak in second place and make it to a primary.

After the first round, those who received fewer votes are knocked out. A second round of speeches are given by candidates, and then another round of voting takes place. The delegates who voted for the eliminated candidates are now up for grabs, so a whole lot of horse-trading happens to secure their votes.

After the first round, I was still in the game. But then it seemed that the "good ol' boys" network was going to win the day. Many elected officials started lining up to endorse and get behind Carl Wimmer. Again, I didn't seem to belong.

I spoke from the heart in the short second-round speech. Carl Wimmer said to go with a proven conservative and then turned the mic over to those who were endorsing him. The attorney general for the State of Utah, Mark Shurtleff, then took the mic and encouraged delegates to vote for a proven conservative, not a token or novelty candidate.

For a nanosecond I thought, "I really don't belong." Then I heard the delegates groan and boo at the attorney general's statement. There was a flurry of activity behind the scenes as the second round of voting began. I will get to that later in the book.

As Mark Shurtleff walked off the stage, Dave Owen, my communications consultant, turned to National Committee member Enid Mickelsen and asked her, "Did you hear what Shurtleff said?" She hadn't. Dave whispered in her ear, and Enid responded with an incredulous "He did what?"

That was all we heard. I was ready to jump into the fray, but Jason pulled me back and said, "No, let them take care of it." Enid threw on her heels because she had taken her shoes off backstage. She went up to Shurtleff, who was at least twice her size, and launched into a barrage of "Who do you think you are?" Pointing her finger in his chest, she continued, "What do you think you are doing? You're finished here. Everyone's gonna see who you are. You are done! Pack your bags. You will always be known as *that guy*."

In that moment, Enid demonstrated as a national GOP leader and former Republican member of Congress that I did indeed belong. And I had someone who not only thought I belonged but would have my back! That was incredibly powerful and empowering for me.

When the tally came in, I had well exceeded the 60 percent threshold, and I became the Republican nominee for the Fourth Congressional District to face Democrat Jim Matheson in the general election. As important as winning—and even avoiding a primary—was, the clear message from the delegates that I did belong meant the most to me.

And that brought me back to when I was backstage in Tampa. It gave me some confidence that perhaps there was a place for me and that perhaps I did have something to say that would bring people together. Maybe, just maybe, I did belong.

In many ways, I felt that I had been thrown into the middle of an Olympic competition with *zero* training for the event I was about to compete in. The lofty hopes of many weighed heavily on my shoulders; I knew their hopes were riding on my ability to deliver. Such moments can be confidence-crushing.

In such moments I often heard the words of my parents preaching hope and confidence from the pulpit of my memory. I remember my parents saying that what they loved most about America was that America believes in dreams, especially in the dreams of the underdog. America loves a great David and Goliath story.

In the America we know, David really can beat Goliath—whether David is a small-town basketball team, an upstart entrepreneur, or a young child who dares to dream.

My favorite line in that biblical story says that David *ran* to meet Goliath. Think of that...He *ran* toward a seemingly impossible challenge. David faced his own moments of doubt and feeling unqualified. In receiving his charge to go face Goliath, he responded by saying he was just a kid—young, unlearned, and inexperienced. The feelings were surely multiplied when the king laughed at the audacious declaration that David would defeat Goliath not with swords and shield and armor, but with a sling. David's brothers chimed in by reminding him that he didn't belong anywhere but back with the sheep.

David walked past those who declared him unqualified and mocked his moxie, and he stepped onto the battlefield. Goliath joined the chorus of jeers, saying that he would feed David's dead and defeated body to the birds.

At every turn of the journey, David could have, and perhaps should have, run in the opposite direction. By any and every measure, he really didn't belong in the battle and was not qualified to stand as the representative of the kingdom.

And yet, David ran!

I would note that the qualified confidence that enabled David to run toward Goliath is also the kind of confidence we need to have as we take on the Goliaths of America's problems: debt, immigration reform, health care, supply chain issues, energy, the economy, and the Godzilla we call Washington bureaucracy. It is time for all of us—for "we the people"—to *run* toward the challenges of our day, not away from them.

Running.

In that cavernous hall back in 2012 at the RNC, I did have thoughts of running. Mostly, I was thinking about running for the exit. Even though I knew I was prepared, my mind was spinning.

So, I ran for the most secluded spot available to me—a bathroom stall in the dressing room. In that less than ideal space, I offered the most heartfelt prayer of my life. And yes, it is possible to offer up an earnest prayer in a bathroom stall while trying not to throw up on your perfectly pressed suit or smudge your makeup. That stall was my haven in the final moments before I had to take the stage. For a moment I was reengaging all the "unqualified" and "you don't belong" doubts I had ever entertained. "Run away, you don't belong" is a haunting phrase and a devastating feeling.

I prayed from the depths of my soul to be able to deliver my message, to not fall in my high heels, that I wouldn't pass out, or that the stage manager wouldn't cut my mic and haul me off the platform if I spoke too long (which he threatened to do during the rehearsal). "Breathe!"

Then my prayer shifted from my insecurities, doubts, and fears to something higher. I didn't want the moment to be about me. I just wanted to be a voice. The words in my mind—"Not my will but Yours"—sunk deep. Kneeling in that backstage bathroom stall, I realized several fundamental truths:

1. I had a story that mattered.
2. I had a voice.
3. The principles I knew, believed, and strived to live were the core of my character.
4. My character qualified me for this moment—I belonged!
5. I was going to mount that stage and raise not just my voice, but the voice of every person who ever hoped to live the American Dream. My voice would be their voice.
6. It was time to run toward the moment.

With my high heels digging into the spongy floor, with "We Will Rock You" blaring as my walk-on music, I strode to the podium to speak my truth: that the America I knew was founded on the unifying principles of freedom and built by humble, hopeful, extraordinary people.

Looking out into that sea of still mostly white faces—and far too many cowboy hats—I suddenly began to feel a sense of belonging. I saw my campaign-color orange towels being waved enthusiastically by the delegates from Utah! The red, white, and blue signs and the flags and banners of patriotic people extended as far as I could see.

I recognized that I wasn't scanning the audience to

see someone like me; they all were like me. I saw the audience for who they were—Americans. I belonged.

I had a story to tell, so I began:

Let me tell you about the America I know. My parents immigrated to the U.S. with ten dollars in their pocket, believing that the America they had heard about really did exist. When times got tough they didn't look to Washington, they looked within.

So the America I came to know was centered in personal responsibility and filled with the American Dream.

The America I know is grounded in the determination found in patriots and pioneers, in small business owners with big ideas, in the farmers who work in the beauty of our landscape, in our heroic military and Olympians. It's in every child who looks at the seemingly impossible and says, "I can do that." That is the America I know!

I continued:

The American Dream isn't just my story and it isn't just your story—it is our story. It is a story of human struggle, standing up and striving for more. It's been told for over 200 years with small steps and giant leaps; from a woman on a bus to a man with a dream; and the bravery of the greatest generation, to the entrepreneurs of today.

This is our story. This is the America we know because we built it.

The crowd erupted in unison. Chants of "U-S-A" rose, echoed, and reverberated throughout the arena. The moment was a miracle to me. In all the cheering and chants I felt an incredible stillness and oneness with all who were listening, seen and unseen. Every thought of being unqualified and not belonging was blasted into oblivion.

I recognized the voice I was attempting to raise was no longer my own. I was united with the crowd. The shared principles of the American story we all longed for and believed in rose in crescendo as I concluded:

We can restore the America we know and love. The world will know it, our children will tell it and our grandchildren will possess it for years to come!

The rest was a blur. I remember the sea of smiling faces. I recall the thunderous applause as I concluded.

As I turned to walk off the stage, I knew who I was: Mia Love—Black, female, conservative Republican, spouse, mother, mayor, daughter of inspiring immigrants, American—qualified by the content of my character.

Boyd met me backstage and described what was happening in the greenroom during my speech: "The greenroom was a 'who's-who' of the Republican Party elite. Very little attention was being paid to the many screens around the room during the previous speakers. There was a lot of glad-handing, hugs, and chatter going on about how great it was for everyone to be in Tampa for the National Convention. A sentence into Mia's speech and the entire room went pin-drop silent. Everyone was leaning in and hanging on every word. Many mouthed the word 'WOW' to each other as the speech progressed and built into a magnificent crescendo. The moment Mia ended, Kevin McCarthy declared, 'That was the speech of the night!'"

The next several days were filled with high-pressure meetings, media availability, and interviews. I was now being proclaimed as a rising star in the GOP. I had gone from wondering if I belonged to being part of the hope for a better future. Belonging came with a little whiplash and even some self-doubt about whether or not it was all real. There were important moments during the course of that convention that gave me the answer to the ultimate question about who we are, what we believe, what we stand for, and what we are willing to do in order to make a difference.

We can all begin our journey toward owning our story and finding our voice with the sense of belonging that comes from answering the question, "Who am I?"

When we recognize that we are qualified and clearly belong, we can then run toward the biggest of life's challenges and be ready to meet with confidence life's most meaningful moments.

CHAPTER 2

Owning Your Story

Everyone has a story. Sometimes that story can feel like a tragedy. Many feel the need to hide their story for fear of what others might think about who they are, where they come from, or where their story might fit on social media platforms.

You may wonder about your story. I did. Early on in my life, I had serious worries about my origin story. It was confusing and troubling to my young mind.

My family and I lived on 20 Novak Street in South Norwalk, Connecticut, in 1986. This was my home in America—where my story began. The house was three stories high, and we actually rented out the top two floors to others. My parents, my two siblings, and I lived on the bottom floor. It was a beautiful house that was always crowded.

One of my earliest memories, and one of the longest lasting lessons I learned from my mother, happened when Mom picked me up from prekindergarten one day. At great personal sacrifice my parents had somehow gotten me into a pre-K prep class at the old Marvin Elementary School. There weren't very many of those opportunities in those days. It was one of many commitments and sacrifices my parents made in order to give me a chance at the American Dream.

I remember one afternoon my mom came to pick me up from school. I am sure Mom was in the midst of another long and exhausting day of work and making ends meet. My mom was holding my hand, while getting after me for a few things as we walked toward the car. She was having one of those moments where her accent might have been a little bit too thick, and maybe she spoke a little too loud. I was annoyed and maybe a little bugged that she didn't look like every other mother, that she didn't sound like every other mother. So, I ripped my hand out of her hand, and I ran toward the car, which was parked across the street.

Seeing me run into the street, my mom yelled and immediately raced after me. As I looked back, I saw her fall onto the pavement. I sprinted across the street and hopped into the car where my brother and sister were waiting. When Mom got into the car, she gave me this incredible look of relief. She didn't scold me. Mom simply sighed deeply, closed her eyes, and exhaled.

I looked at my mom's knees. They were both dripping with blood.

I remember asking her, "Why did you run after me? Why did you run after me?" Mom very softly replied, "I didn't want you to get hit by a car."

I felt so bad. And I felt something else too. I saw and felt at that moment the love and the fears and all of the other emotions that a mother has for her child. I recognized that my mom, with her loud voice and thick accent, loved me as much, if not more, than all the other mothers loved the other kids that went to my school.

I knew that there wasn't a thing Mom wouldn't do for me—ever. Mom was definitely different. Uniquely different. Powerfully different. She was qualified to be my mother. She was more than qualified to raise someone who was going to do something special. I would draw on her love and commitment to me in crucial moments throughout my life.

I remember one day in December when we were cleaning the house to get ready for a very special occasion, my birthday party. But this was not just any birthday party—this was going to be my first "normal" birthday party. I was turning eleven years old, and my one wish was that I could have a normal party with real invitations to hand out to friends from my school, lots of food, fun, and games.

In the Haitian community, birthdays were always causes for big celebrations. Family members, friends, and neighbors would come over and fill the house beyond its capacity. It seemed that Mama and Daddy knew the whole world and provided a space for all to come. That commitment to create a space for all to come has been a principle I have tried to apply in meeting with constituents, bringing opposing groups together, welcoming my children's friends to our home, and when learning about those who think or believe differently from me.

When it came to the people at our parties at 20 Novak Street, we often weren't sure about who was invited and who just came. Some of the people at the family parties would show up, and we couldn't even figure out if we were related. Often on my December birthday there would be many people who would show up that didn't even know it was my birthday; they simply came for Mama's cooking or Daddy's liquor.

My eleventh birthday was going to be different. I handed out thirty proper invitations to the kids at school. I didn't really know many of the kids in my neighborhood. Mom and Dad kept us busy at school with activities and afterschool programs. My parents didn't want us coming home alone while they were still at work. I was very excited after distributing proper invitations for my proper birthday party.

On the day of my birthday party, I was busy helping mom prepare the finger food, carefully instructing her to make "normal" food that my friends would recognize, like hot dogs and pizza. I was dreaming of slow-dancing with Derek Easton and having a house full of my own friends as Kool and the Gang cassette tapes played in the background.

As five o'clock came, I waited expectantly. After I had waited nearly three hours, my friend Tom Abrahamson walked in the door and handed me my one and only gift of the night. He quickly informed me that he could only stay a few minutes. His parents were waiting for him in the driveway.

I was confused and told him to stay longer, insisting that my parents could drive him home. But he said the only reason he came was because he had made me a personal promise to come. He informed me that I lived in the most dangerous place in Norwalk. No other parents from school would be letting their kids come to my neighborhood.

It was a very sad and disconcerting eleventh birthday. I wondered what was wrong with me. I wanted to believe I belonged. Finally, I realized for the first time that I lived in what some might call "the ghetto."

My story had started in my home. Now it seemed that my home, and all who lived in it, didn't belong.

Not knowing is especially unnerving, particularly when you're a young girl trying to fit in. I will never forget one day I went with my mom to the store to get groceries and a few other things. I can still see the sign for Riverview Plaza in South Norwalk, Connecticut. It was a tiny little run-down strip mall. Inside the strip mall was the Pathmark store. It was like a "Savers" store and was where the poorest of the poor went to get "generic brands" and discount items. I remember getting bargain basement shoes, clothes, and food there over the years. It was just the place we went, and I didn't think about what it meant, or how it was different, until this particular day with my mom.

Our shopping cart was not filled with much when we approached the cereal aisle. On that day I remember seeing brand-name cereals from Kellogg's and other companies—real-life "sugar" cereals that all the other kids got to have every morning. I spotted the Apple Jacks and instantly knew that I just had to have them. I remember grabbing the box and running over to my mom asking if I could put it in the cart. Mom said a very emphatic "No!"

I immediately started to beg my mom to please, please, please let me have them just this one time. The battle was on. I dug in and so did my mother. As the battle of wills continued, my mom said with her very thick Haitian accent, "Mia, the answer is *no*—I have no money!"

Mom then grabbed a big box of generic brand corn flakes and a big bag of puffed wheat.

I wasn't finished. I took one more swing at making my case for the Apple Jacks. At that moment a few of my friends from school happened to walk by. My mom now yelled in her distinctive way, "Mia, I told you I don't have money for that!"

Few things are worse for a young girl than to have your mom yell at you in front of your friends. This was worse because she not only yelled, as only she could yell, in front of my friends—but it was also in a very public place in front of many others with the message that we were too poor to belong.

Fight-or-flight kicked into my young mind, and I decided it was time to run. As I ran away my mother yelled even louder, drawing even more attention. The louder she got the more distinct her accent became. I felt the tears welling up. Then my mind started racing. And so did my feet. I started to run. I paused for a moment, thinking about the consequences of running. My mother was not happy, and she was getting angrier by the moment. Between the embarrassment and the potential consequences bouncing in my scared brain, I decided that whatever the punishment might be, it would be worth it just to get out of that moment.

I was certain this scene was going to be talked about all over school. I kept running. My mom kept yelling. She got louder until finally I was out of the store and into the parking lot. I got to our car and hunkered down beside it. I was so embarrassed. I didn't belong. I was certain I would be teased the next day at school or looked down upon as the girl with the mom who had no money, not even for cereal.

I waited for what seemed like forever. The longer my mom took, the worse I thought the punishment was going to be, and the more worried I became about what the kids at school were going to say. My mom finally came to the car.

Mom said little as she put the groceries in the car. She handed me a minibox of Apple Jacks.

My children love to hear this story about their mom and grandmother. Each time I tell it, my kids jump in and say, "If Grandma was yelling at me in a store like that, I would run too!"

———————

Sometimes you just have to get lucky.

Sometimes in America hard work and taking a chance produce some luck. I was not quite sixteen and so anxious to get my driver's license, even though I knew I would have few opportunities to actually drive because my parents needed the car to drive to work.

My dad worked as a janitor at Our Lady of Fatima Catholic School. Late one Saturday night the phone rang, and I rushed over and answered it. It was someone from the school who wanted to talk to my dad. I remember wondering why in the world the school would be calling late on a Saturday. I even asked the person why they were calling my dad.

The man on the phone said, "I just want you to know that you just won a brand-new car." I assumed it was a prank. The man repeated, "If you want a brand-new car, you have to come and get it at the school tonight."

I was just about to hang up. The man, a little exasperated, said, "Please let me talk to your dad!" My dad had just walked in the house, so I gave him the phone. In about three seconds he started screaming, jumping up and down, and shouting, "We won a new car!"

It was the school fund-raiser, and my dad had purchased a raffle ticket for $25.

I couldn't believe it. "Dad, since when do you buy raffle tickets? I had asked for money for a sandwich, you only gave me like five bucks, but you're out buying raffle tickets?"

Dad grabbed my hand, and we hopped in our car. We drove over to this event, and sure enough, there we see this beautiful cherry-red, brand-new Chevrolet Beretta!

I held his hand tight and called him Daddy. I said it very sweetly, very deliberately, very liberally. Deep down, of course, I didn't think I was going to get the Beretta. But you know, we paid the taxes, which was really hard for our family.

A few days later, I happened to pass my driver's test with flying colors. And so Daddy let me drive to my practices in the brand-new Beretta. Eventually, it ended up becoming my car. I learned that working hard and taking a chance once in a while can make you lucky. Mostly, I was lucky to have parents who usually created their own luck.

Owning your story starts with owning your origin story. It took me years to recognize the love of family, the power of community, and the principles I learned in a priceless place some people were absolutely unwilling to come to.

There were some who did come. They changed me and my story forever.

When I was in junior high, this group of amazing girls from the high school used to come around. The girls were part of the color guard from our high school, and they were recognized as perennial champions. They started having a junior high color guard. They would let us younger girls go and perform in parades with them. I remember just really liking these girls. They were so cool, and to have the chance to do something like color guard with them was amazing. I desperately wanted to do something compelling and challenging, and I so wanted to be part of something—a winning story.

At that point in junior high, I had retreated to the role of always being the team manager but never really on the team. I remember just taking up the flag and becoming part of the color guard family. These older girls were really a big influence on my story and what I wanted to become.

I will forever remember when they said, "Mia, you should try out for the color guard." They meant at the high school—the championship-winning high school color guard!

There was a spirit and a culture on that color guard that transcended the performances and championships. It was pretty intense. I remember meeting Jeff Smith, who was the band director, and he was intense. From the very beginning he said, "We own you. We practice three hours every day, except for Saturdays. We practice from 8 a.m. to 5 p.m. at night in the summer, if we don't have competition."

The list of other requirements was long. It included our school classwork. In order to play a sport or be part of anything in the high school, you had to have a 2.5 GPA. That was simply not good enough for Jeff Smith. He required a 3.0 or above, period. He would insist that the band and color guard were never going to be satisfied with doing just the bare minimum. So we had to do well in school. That was what he required. That was what he expected. It was a high-energy, time-consuming commitment that at times was crazy.

There was one more crazy commitment—money! Uniforms, flags, and travel were significant commitments. We didn't have any money for such things. I vividly remember going to Jeff and explaining that my parents didn't have money to pay for uniforms, flags, and all of those things. Without hesitation Jeff told me that if I worked hard, I didn't need to worry about any of that stuff. He frankly said that he would handle it. He reminded me that he required nothing but perfection—at least perfect effort, focus, commitment, and energy.

Having someone say—and show—that they believed in you, not because it was their job, but because they saw you and your potential is life-changing. That sense of belonging is priceless. There is nothing like being part of a winning story, whether it is a color guard, a sports team, a campaign, a community, or a country—a shared story is transformational.

The color guard story was intense, and the pressure it produced was high. Because of the demanding practices and schedule, I didn't have time to procrastinate. I didn't have time to get in much trouble. I'd run home, have an hour to myself after I got home, then get ready to go to practice. There simply was no time to play around or put things off to get done later. By the time I would return home from practice I was completely exhausted. I learned to maximize that hour, because when I was so ready to collapse and go to sleep, the last thing I wanted to do was open up a book. I had an hour to get whatever I needed to get done. I not only developed the discipline to study during that hour but I also learned how to study well—a skill I have used throughout my life and career.

Even after becoming part of a success story like our championship-winning color guard, there were still regular old lessons to be learned—including some humility.

My first crush was in band. My first embarrassing moment followed soon after. Mr. Smith had strict rules during practice. If you messed up, you had to run laps. For color guard, that meant running laps in a skirt. Now these skirts where thick, long, and heavy, and actually had wooden dowels in them so we could twirl them around during our routines.

Once during a practice, I did something wrong, so Mr. Smith told me I needed to run around the parking lot with two friends of mine. I am pretty sure we messed each other up, so it was probably appropriate that we had to run together.

We started running, and I saw the kid that I had a crush on, Jimmy—who was one of the hotshot guys and a snare drum player—on the drumline. I tried to be cool. I was running and running (always running, it seems), and as I was running I tripped over a dowel in the skirt.

In perhaps my least graceful moment of all time I went tumbling head-over-heels, and the dowel stuck me in places that I'm not going to mention. It was a very humbling moment for me.

We would go to these band and color guard trips, and I wouldn't have very much money—which was always a point of worry and stress for me. There were so many kids that had money. Mr. Smith would say, "Don't worry, Miss Bourdeau—everything will be fine."

While the other kids were walking around with $200 that their parents gave them, I usually only had $20—if I was lucky—that my parents would scrape together for me at the last minute. We went to perform at the Rose Bowl twice, and both times I was there with just $20. Mr. Smith would tell my mom that the school was paying for the food and that I really didn't need any more than $20.

My mom recognized what it meant for me to be part of this winning story on color guard. She would stay up late and wait for the band buses to come—sometimes it was 3 a.m., but she was there waiting. She always supported my doing this. Because I got great grades, I focused and began to believe in my story and that there was a place I belonged.

In fact, one time a friend of mine quit the band. She was burned out, just didn't want to do it, disliked the time commitment, and really just wanted to play. Not long after she quit, she was out one day with her friends. They got into a horrible accident. I was actually in a band competition at the time. My mom went to the hospital to make sure my friend was going to be all right. My friend's mother said something I'll never forget. She told my mom, "It's important for your kids to not be idle and to be doing things."

My mom went to be with her because she was a former band mom. Band parents form an amazing bond; they actually have their own story. My friend's mom told my mom that if her daughter had not quit, her daughter would not have been in the hospital that day, and she would have been waiting in that parking lot with the other parents for their kids to return.

Mom told me that day that when I had my own kids, I should not let them be idle, but help them find something to do that they can do well so they can use their gifts and talents.

I learned how to work hard and appreciate that a good work ethic was a priceless commodity by being in the band and color guard. This was where I learned to be nervous but still perform at my best. I came to understand that practice makes permanent, and that perfect practice makes perfect. You really do get out of a performance what you put into practice.

My story began in a place where funds were scarce and economic stress was real, but where I knew I belonged.

Rather than be ashamed of my geography and economy, I learned to embrace the diversity and the powerful lessons I was taught by people—family, neighbors, and newfound friends who loved me and ultimately touched and shaped the story I now own.

My story is deeply rooted in the American Dream. I actually love the idea that America really shouldn't be a melting pot but instead should be a salad bowl. I do love a good salad! The salad bowl is really quite instructive because the ingredients, while coming together, never lose their identities or stories. The tomato remains a tomato, the crispness of the cucumber continues, the flavor of the onions does not disappear, and the color of carrots stays bright. The lettuce doesn't need to hide itself, and the spinach doesn't need to transform into a blueberry. Each of the ingredients keeps its unique story; the ingredients do not try to become something else, something they are not.

We need more of that in America; there is still far too much division present in America.

I learned a most extraordinary lesson in owning my story from my oldest daughter, Alessa. She worked herself into becoming a phenomenal basketball player. Even though she jumped on the court later than most female basketball athletes do, she just got it. The game was in her.

She understood it, she felt it, and she was really, really good at it.

There was a young girl who had been Alessa's teammate for some time. This girl had been playing basketball alongside Alessa in practice and games and knew my daughter well. One day, in the middle of a drill during practice, she turned to Alessa and declared, "Well, you know why you're good at basketball, right? It's because you're Black. You have an advantage."

Alessa's reaction to that was "Oh, thank you!" When the girl was surprised by her reaction, Alessa explained, "You pretty much called me superhuman!" Alessa concluded the exchange by saying, "And guess what? I run really fast, too."

Alessa walked away from that moment feeling empowered, rather than inferior or degraded. Whether that girl meant it as an insult or was trying to make her feel ashamed, Alessa chose to see it as a compliment.

Owning her story gave my daughter power and confidence. Alessa saw her biracial qualities as an asset, so when the girl called it out, she agreed! Alessa leaned into both her races and appreciated her multicultural heritage.

After this experience, which could have caused Alessa to question her own story and whether she belonged, she instead decided to tryout for track, and she excelled there as well.

I am trying to teach my children and empower others

to see their differences as strengths, to be proud of who they are. I am teaching my children to be proud of their African heritage and Scottish-Hispanic heritage because there are advantages in all of it. All of it.

When we value and own our personal stories, we are in a position to lift others up to see their unique stories, heritage, backgrounds, and qualities as benefits. Knowing who you are and being proud of it is essential to becoming confidently qualified. Each of our stories is valuable, however different each may be. Our stories prove that it is by the content of our character that we can and must be measured.

Owning my story is what propelled me to become the only Republican member of the Congressional Black Caucus. Taking a seat at the table gave me the opportunity to work across the political aisle on many issues that appeared divisive but could actually be solved by valuing the differences in each other. Sharing our stories with others and being confident enough to take a seat at the table and raise our voices is what our nation needs most.

As I began to see the importance and power of my own heritage and story, the people around me encouraged me to share it with others. The avenue I found for that message was a position in politics. The world of politics was a way I found for my story to have a direct impact on the nation I love. When we own our stories, we empower others to do the same. That makes all of us better.

New York Times best-selling author Joseph Grenny has done a great deal of work over the years in South Africa. Joseph noted that in the nation's regular polling of its people regarding race relations there is one question that could transform everything. The question? "In the last six months have you had someone from another race over for lunch or dinner?"[1]

If each of us had someone different from us over for lunch or dinner—or simply interacted with people who didn't look like, believe like, or live like we do—every six months, imagine the insight such interactions could create and the difference they could make!

When I was in high school, I got a job teaching swimming lessons. I really loved teaching. I felt like I was making a difference for these kids, especially those who were just starting out. If they could just learn the basics, it could mean the difference between life and death, and it could open up a whole new world for them.

I had one little boy in my class who took quite a long time to pick things up. Even just getting his face in the water to blow bubbles was a struggle. My goal was to always get the kids to trust me so that they could develop the skills to trust themselves and have confidence in the water.

Eventually, things started to click for this little boy. I will never forget the day he put his head down in the water and he swam the length of the pool to where I was waiting and encouraging him.

When he got to me, he threw his arms around my neck and squeezed and held on so tight. He was so pleased and proud of his accomplishment. Then he said, "You know, my parents say that Black people are really bad. But I don't believe them, and I don't care what they say—I really like you!"

It was the first time that it had occurred to me that racism or hatred is taught and learned. Even though we may have a natural inclination to gravitate toward people who are like us, gravitating toward someone is very different from turning away from someone. That little boy taught me a priceless lesson: Your example and your relationships can make a difference.

When we engage in personal relationships, we transcend politics, biases, and obstacles. I think that should extend beyond race to political perspectives, lifestyle choices, faith, and more. Imagine if we all were willing to lean in and listen to someone else's story. Learning from and embracing the story of those who look, think, believe, and live differently than we do would go a long way toward bridging divides and uniting the nation.

My story is a personal witness that the inequality of the often-underrepresented stories of Americans doesn't have to determine destiny. My hope is that as we embrace our own stories, we will be spurred to action and feel empathy for the stories of others. Rather than accepting that this is the way things are—that this is the way they have always been and this is the way they will be in the future—we can become agents of change.

With my eyewitness view of my parents' dream for a better life in America, I knew that change and a better future was possible through hard work and determination. Beginnings don't equal endings in the American story. Your geography cannot contain the content of your character.

I recognized that I grew up in what most people would call a ghetto of America, but I developed a determination to strive for a better life for myself. I did not allow my humble background to deter me from my chances of success. Rather than the beginning of my story determining the ending, I was inspired to passionately pursue the opportunity to write my own story.

I chose to believe in and own for myself the promise of the American Dream. This is my story. I invite you to explore and own your story. Owning your story is the beginning of discovering the content of your character and the foundation for your confidence that you are indeed qualified.

CHAPTER 3

You Have a Voice— Raise It!

While I have always had a voice, it has taken a lifetime for me to understand my voice and how to properly raise it.

As a child I loved to sing—loudly! I would walk around the house belting out, "The sun will come out tomorrow!" My siblings teased me relentlessly over my constant, crank-it-up-to-11 singing of that song. I think they might have wondered if the sun wouldn't come out due to my singing.

There was something about music and song that

touched me deeply and stirred me greatly. I felt more alive, more happy, more me when I was using my voice.

In elementary school I realized I was different from the other students. In particular, I discovered that I learned in a way that was foreign to most of my classmates. I was blessed with a most amazing teacher, Miss Giriglia. She was not content with just moving through the curriculum or even merely ensuring students could pass tests. She was determined to empower each of us to do what we do best, to learn in a way that worked for us, and above all, to learn to love learning.

Miss Giriglia discovered that I learned things really easily through song. Matching music, my voice, and a message—even if it was about science or math or English—produced real results. I still remember getting ready for a quiz where I had to name all of the prepositions. Miss Giriglia said, "Mia, just put them in a song." I did just that, and I can still sing them all today. My teacher recognized that I was like a mega-memorizing monster when I put something to song. So that was how she taught me. Miss Giriglia helped me use my voice to learn things that were vital for my education and my future. She saw me as unique and was unwilling to let me flounder. Instead, she helped me to flourish.

But I was still a shy, unconfident elementary-school girl, and Miss Giriglia wasn't finished with me yet. She had plans to help me discover and use my voice in other ways. She had me volunteer at a nearby convalescent home. I loved it. I got to go over to the home during one period in school. I met all of these amazing older people who all seemed to love me for who I was, not who I wasn't.

The home would pair me up with the older residents who needed somebody like me. In particular, they would pair me up with people who either didn't have children or didn't have children or grandchildren who would come to visit them very often. I became the little girl they all loved like their own. In the process, I recognized my voice mattered to them.

In fact, there was one wonderful woman that would literally repeat everything I said. I would wheel her around the facility and greet all the other residents. I would say, "What's up, man?" and she would parrot, "What's up, man?" I would say things in different ways, "How's it going down?" And she would follow with the same emphasis, "How's it going down?" Then we would all laugh.

Laughter is an important part of our voices that we often neglect as we get older. This older woman loved to repeat my voice, and I loved her for loving my voice. She and I would play ball with the other residents in their chairs. I would take time and paint her nails. She liked it.

I loved using my voice to care and be there for these

older people who didn't have anybody else. I felt that they wanted me there. I loved visiting them. I had such a good time doing it, and in the end I am certain I got more out of the experience than those I was there to serve. I learned that every voice matters. I was young, and my voice mattered. Many of them were old and had lost their ability to give voice to all they knew and all they had experienced. Their voices and fading memories echoed in my heart and would later become part of a visual that drove much of my work when I found my own voice in Congress. It was an image of those voices I needed to protect, promote, and serve—the yet to be born and the soon to depart.

Miss Giriglia recognized how much I loved this, how it was giving me confidence in my voice, so she would always work with the school administrators to make sure they would give me that one period where I could go over to the center and spend time with the residents.

One day after I had returned from the elderly center Miss Giriglia told me I had been nominated for a very special service award from the J. C. Penney Company. She said she would like for my mom to come. I got a day off from school to go, and my mom and this very special teacher came with me to the award ceremony.

The J. C. Penney award was part of a program the company did in conjunction with donations it made to senior centers and convalescent centers. The awards were a way for J. C. Penney to honor those who volunteered or provided special services to the senior citizens of the community. My teacher pointed out that I was part of the award program and would be recognized with some kind of honor.

The event began, and they started going through and giving awards to various people; some were adults and some were children. As things went along, I started to get a little nervous and maybe even a little embarrassed as my name hadn't been called. I wondered if there was a mistake and maybe I wasn't really supposed to be there.

The longer it went the more I was wondering, "What am I doing here?" I even got a little frustrated, thinking, "We got all dressed up for this!"

Miss Giriglia must have sensed my concern. At one point she leaned over to me and said, "You know, the further down you go the bigger the award. You are going to get one of the biggest awards. There aren't very many left."

Next thing I knew, the person sitting at our table was given a $1,000 award. My mom's eyes got big, and she softly said, "You mean we're gonna get more than $1,000?" Miss Giriglia replied, "Yes, you're going to get more than $1,000." Then they announced the $2,000 award. They announced the $3,000 award, and then the $4,000 award. My name still hadn't been called.

As they got ready to announce the final award, I could literally feel my mom's legs shaking. My mom was trying to keep herself together while whispering in broken English, "Oh, my gosh, so much we're gonna do with this!" Miss Giriglia patted me on the shoulder, exclaiming, "It's you, Mia. You're the only one left. It has to be you!"

The nice man running the show then said into the microphone, "Our final award is for Mia Bourdeau for her excellent volunteering and the love she has shown to a special group of our senior citizens." He explained that they were surprised that I had been nominated by so many people, and he read the names of all who had nominated me. He read many of their notes and why my voice and my service had changed their lives. The woman who would always repeat what I said as I wheeled her around the facility wrote, "I am so grateful when I wake up in the morning on the days Mia is coming." It was so sweet and so surprising to me.

They called me up to the front of the room. I got up there, and there was this great big check for $5,000. They told me, "We're so excited. And we'd like to offer this to you for your excellent service." They explained that it was part of a special endowment from the J. C. Penney Company for the community. They mentioned that there was a long-standing tradition involving how the award money would be used.

I could see my mom just beaming. My mom had not had any idea that she would be walking in to a $5,000 check. For us, that amount of money wasn't just a big deal; it was a game changer. My mom was a housekeeper. My dad cleaned toilets as a janitor.

Then in an instant, the bomb dropped, and the game-changing check changed. The ceremony was being broadcast live on local TV. They said, "Mia, we are so thankful for you and are glad you are part of that long-standing tradition. Because Mia is so committed to service, she will do what our previous top award winners have done—Mia will sign over the check to the convalescent home!" There were cheers and applause.

However, my mom would not let go of that check. I nudged her, "Mom, you have to let go. We have to give it back. We are on TV." I pulled the check away from my mom and handed it over.

My mom was a bit shaken as we went back to our seats. After she regained her composure, she said, "I had already spent that money in my head." She began to list all the things on her spending list from shoes and sneakers, to home repairs, clothes, some debts to be paid, along with a litany of other things she had longed for but had never been able to afford. Then it was over.

That J. C. Penney award is still sitting on the mantel at my mom's house, and it reminds her of that $5,000 she saw but was never able to spend. It was indeed the biggest award of the day, and we have often joked that it would have been better to come in second place and keep the $4,000 than to win the grand prize and give the $5,000 back!

Of course, the real lesson—and the priceless prize— was the realization that my voice truly mattered and could make a difference in the lives of others, especially the most vulnerable.

———————

Mark and Donna McKenzie lived in the same city of Norwalk, Connecticut. My sister would get to know them well and babysit their kids, and the same happened for me. Donna made the best lasagna. And she became like a second mom to me and my sister. I asked her to go prom dress shopping with me, and we saw this dress. I put it on, and it was beautiful. We looked at the price tag. We both instantly knew that there was no way my parents could afford such a dress for a prom.

Donna said, "I'm buying this for you."

I replied, "No, you can't do that."

She said, "Mia, I'm buying this for you. You've done really well in school, Mark and I want to help and support your mom, and I'm going to buy this dress for you."

The McKenzies became an incredible support. They became part of my village. To this day we're still very close. The McKenzies would tell me all the time that I was going to grow up and do something big. They believed in me, and I started to believe them. They took us on family trips. My first trip to Disney World was with Mark and Donna. They loved me and my sister, Cyndi, like their own children. The world would be an amazing place if everyone had a Mark and Donna in their lives. Cyndi and I were blessed.

When I reached high school, I put my voice back to work when I joined the choir. Nothing too great, nothing too grand—just a plain old member of the most basic choir.

Then one day in class Mrs. Hall made a comment I doubt she would have remembered, but one that changed my life forever. She said, "You have a pretty voice. You should try out to be in the chamber choir."

Mrs. Hall's observation was transformational. Someone besides me, my imaginary friends, and the stuffed animals on my bed had recognized I had a voice. I auditioned and was chosen to be in the chamber choir, and opportunities to learn about, improve, and share my voice began to come quickly. Soon I was presented with the chance to be in a real musical—*Barnum*.

I was cast as the 102-year-old lady and had my own song, "Thank God I'm Old." I had developed a pretty decent "big belt" that resonated in this song, and people responded. I remember the gym teacher coming up to me after the first performance and saying, "Mia, you have a gift from God." She told me she didn't even like musicals but came to every performance to hear my voice.

Comments like that from people outside of my family validated me and sparked a desire to push my voice as far as possible. I ultimately ended up in *West Side Story* my senior year of high school. I applied to the University of Hartford's Hartt School of Music and received a half-tuition scholarship for the fall of 1993.

The faculty members at Hartford were extraordinary. While I knew I had a voice, I really didn't understand what that meant or could mean. While on campus, I learned that having a voice wasn't enough; you had to do something with it that mattered and would make a difference.

One faculty member who challenged me to own and explore my voice was Peter Flint. He was our teacher of teachers, and sadly, he passed away far too soon—but he is forever a part of my life and the lives of those who were blessed to be tutored by his vision and direction. Peter had a motto for those of us in musical theater. He had us memorize it—but more important, he challenged us to live it.

The motto was, "I am an artist. These are my emotions and I own them. And I like them. My talent comes from something other than myself, but I alone am responsible for it. I will dare to be bad, so that I may be good. I am an artist. I am that I am."

Peter continually challenged each of us to rise up to the best that was within us. He gave us the courage to know it was okay to be bad in the beginning and that working through the bad was the only way to rise to the good and ultimately to the best we had within us. Above all, Peter expected us to take responsibility and ownership for our talents and gifts. The way I viewed my voice began to change.

I learned in classrooms and on the stage in Hartford that in most cases we do not necessarily rise to the occasion; we usually rise to the level of our preparation.

Up to this point in my pursuit of acting and singing and performing, I had gone for the roles that were not necessarily a stretch for me, typecast roles for which I looked the part or at least close to the part. Then Peter shook my world by challenging me not to go for such typecast roles.

Peter said to me, "Mia, don't just accept the part you look like. Take the part you want and make the audience see you as the part!"

If what Peter was telling me was true, I could take any part! I no longer had any limits to what I could explore, pursue, or do. My world went from very small to an unlimited expanse. My voice could take me anywhere.

Far too many in our nation have limited themselves to typecast roles in their schooling, work, careers, relationships, and communities. Far too many have settled for lives of mediocrity, limited by beliefs, stereotypes, self-doubt, and even bias. Some accept that there isn't an American Dream for them because they don't fit the mold or meet the current criteria.

To any who have felt that the die is cast for their future, I say it is time for you to no longer take the typecast role. Go for the role you are needed in and make everyone around you see it. The world needs you to recognize, develop, and use your voice.

My time on campus was really a master class for me in understanding and owning my voice and developing the confidence and skills necessary to rise up and raise my voice in an array of venues.

A few years ago, I was privileged to receive an honorary degree from Hartford and deliver the keynote commencement address at graduation.

I began:

My mind has been racing back to so many places and spaces on this campus; to so many lessons learned, and to so many people who made a difference in my life. My time here as a student stretched me, strengthened me, and positioned me to rise to my full potential.

I then shared with the graduates what has become a favorite quote of mine. It is a quote often attributed to Winston Churchill: "To each there comes...a special moment when they are figuratively tapped on the shoulder and offered the chance to do a very special thing, unique to them and fitted to their talents. What a tragedy if that moment finds them unprepared or unqualified for that which could have been their finest hour."[1]

I challenged the students, saying, "The great question you will face in the days and years ahead is this: 'Am I prepared to rise in such moments?' I hope you consider graduation day the first of many taps on the shoulder that will lead you to a lifetime of finest hours as you rise to the full measure of your potential."

I provided three important principles I had learned on campus that I believed would determine the future for these young graduates—priceless principles for them to keep in mind as they prepared to rise to their utmost potential and raise their voice in their careers and communities.

First, your ability to rise is going to be dependent on your commitment to continuous learning. I know, I know—that is the last thing you want to hear today. But it is true. We live in a world accelerating in fast-forward. We have more changes in one of our twenty-four-hour days than our grandparents had in decades of their lives. Two of the most important things you have picked here in college is learning how to learn [the discipline of learning] and learning to *love* learning. Your success is going to be determined, to a large extent, by what you learn after you leave here today. Rising to the opportunities ahead of you is going to require a lifetime of learning.

Second, your ability to rise will be bolstered or shackled by your ability to engage in elevated dialogue. It may seem crazy for a member of Congress to be talking about elevated dialogue—but I believe it is the key to all of our finest hours. As a nation, as individuals, and as communities, we must get comfortable having uncomfortable conversations.

We cannot rise if we are constantly spewing divisive and demonizing rhetoric. It is so tempting to melt down someone's Twitter feed or blow up their Facebook page with anger-filled words of frustration. Someone wisely said, "Speak in anger and you will give the best speech you ever live to regret." Even if it is a virtual speech on social media, the result is the same. Remember that the solution to any problem begins when someone says, "Let's talk about it." We have a long way to go as a country—but it starts with each of us individually being willing to have an elevated conversation about the challenges of our day. It is impossible to rise without being comfortable and confident in higher dialogue.

Third, remember that your goal is to rise with, not over, others. There is an old Scottish saying, "Thee lift me and I'll lift thee and together we'll ascend." Sadly our society tells us more and more that we should just look out for number one and not worry about anyone else.

I shared my dad's story and how he came to this country with $10 in his pocket in an attempt to rise above the poverty and strife of his native Haiti. Through grit and determination, he and my mom provided me and my siblings with the opportunity to find our voices and rise in pursuit of our own version of the American Dream.

I will always remember the day my dad dropped me off here on campus. He looked me in the eye and said, "Mia, your mom and I have worked hard to provide you the opportunity to rise. You will give back. You will contribute. You will make a difference for others." What he was telling me is that it was part of my responsibility not only to rise myself, but to bring others along with me.

I will confess that stepping onto this campus that day the thought of being a mayor, a mother, or a member of Congress were not remotely in my mind. But when I stepped away from this campus, as each of you will today, I was ready to rise to new roles, responsibilities, and opportunities. Each of those roles has given me an opportunity to learn, to engage in elevated dialogue, and help others rise to their potential.

You are the rising generation. You are the leaders, not just for tomorrow, but for today.

Today I challenge you to raise your sights, not just your status, as you enter the workforce and a world desperately in need of your energy, talent, and commitment.

Remember the second half of the statement attributed to Churchill about those taps on the shoulder and those opportunities to rise: "What a tragedy if that moment finds them unprepared or unqualified for that which could have been their finest hour." Or as John Greenleaf Whittier wrote, "Of all sad words of tongue or pen, the saddest are these: 'It might have been.'"

We cannot accept "what might have been." It is a haunting phrase. Fifty years from now you will have far more regrets about the opportunities you didn't take, the mountains you did not climb, and the adventures you did not pursue than you will ever have for opportunities you took—even when you tried and failed.

When we fail to continuously learn, we will be left to live with what might have been.

When we fail to engage in elevated dialogue in our homes, communities, and places of employment, we will be left to live with what might have been.

When we fail to lift others as we ourselves rise, we will be left to live with what might have been.

Looking back, I recognize that when we fail to acknowledge, develop, and raise our voice, we cannot rise, and we are left with a lifetime of what might have been.

I concluded by challenging the graduates to take their college campus experiences and rise up while raising their voices that are so vital for America's future.

———————

A number of years ago, my family and I were at an event in our community. There was a large hot-air balloon there as part of the fun. An opportunity arose for me to go up in the balloon. As I approached, they told me to bring one of my children along for the ride. I called to my son Peyton, who was seven years old, to come jump in the basket with me. He hesitated and resisted. The balloon was ready to launch, and we couldn't wait for Peyton to decide, so I called to my daughter Abi, who jumped in, and off we went.

After rising in the crisp, cool air and enjoying the amazing view of my district in Utah, we started our return to the ground. As we began to descend, the winds picked up—and let's just say the landing was a bit of an adventure. Peyton had watched all the fun from the ground.

As we got out of the basket, he came running over, shouting that he was ready for his turn. Unfortunately, with the now-windy conditions, the balloon had to stay on the ground. The opportunity to rise and soar in the sky came and was gone.

I took Peyton aside and told him to remember this experience, because in life—especially here in America—if you don't take an opportunity, it quickly passes, and you never know if it will come back. When presented with an opportunity, we must rise to the occasion; we must raise our voices.

I am most thankful for all those who told me, "Mia, you have a voice." Little did I know then that my voice would be raised in the halls of Congress, on the floor of the House of Representatives, on the steps of the Capitol, on national news programs, and in marches on the National Mall.

More important, my voice has been raised in my community, in my children's schools, at VA hospitals, drug treatment centers, senior living facilities, and in my own living room.

Regardless of your background, upbringing, or education, I am here to tell you that you have a voice! Use it!

Raise your voice and you will rise, and you will take those you lead and those you care about to extraordinary heights.

CHAPTER 4

Hinges the Size of Midges

It's been said that the door of history turns on small hinges. The door to my future family and the door to the world of politics opened for me on hinges the size of a gnat, or a midge, as they call the tiny flies that swarm around the lakes of Utah.

During my time at Hartford, I began learning and exploring the world in new and exciting ways. I was most interested in musical theater—because, you know, everything is better in song! I also enjoyed learning about government, politics, and religion. My exploration turned tiny hinges in my mind, my heart, and my soul. I began to understand and galvanize my motivations and spur my passions. In ways that I couldn't even see at the time, other doors of growth and opportunity were being opened on the small hinges of change.

Although I was raised in the Catholic faith, I made the decision during this season of growth and exploration at college to join The Church of Jesus Christ of Latter-day Saints. My faith has always shaped the person I am, driven the difference-maker I want to be, and inspired the influence and impact I want to have on the world and those around me.

One of the things that drew me to The Church of Jesus Christ was the idea that families can be together forever. That stirred my soul. I always knew I wanted to be married and have children. I had experienced what family means for children, neighborhoods, and communities.

I remember hearing one church leader say from the pulpit, in a very commanding voice, "Men, you are to love your wife. You love your wife, like Jesus loves the church. That is the standard. Nothing less than that will ever do."

I thought, "Wow! Yes! I want my husband to love me like that. And they're telling every man from the pulpit that's what they have to do." I knew I needed to marry somebody who would have that kind of commitment. It was a standard that I had never heard in a church before. Combining that commitment with the principle of being married and united as families for time and eternity became my goal. Finding someone to pursue that path with me was about to unfold.

One midge-sized set of hinges I couldn't possibly have imagined turned when I met one of the volunteer missionaries for The Church of Jesus Christ serving in my local congregation. That missionary would one day become my man, my husband, and my partner—Jason Love. If you would have told me at that time that I would marry Jason, move to Utah, and become a member of Congress, I am not sure which of the three I would have thought to be the most crazy and unlikely. There wasn't an instant moment that I knew Jason would be the one for me. Honestly, I thought a lot of the missionaries were handsome and sharing such important lessons with me that I was happy to talk with all of them. It wasn't long after I had been introduced to Elder Love (the title missionaries are given while serving) that Jason finished his two-year mission for the Church and returned home to Utah.

I began working as a flight attendant. One of the great benefits of flying was that I could establish my home wherever I wanted and could work from anywhere. I decided to live in Utah for six months and give it a try. It was during that time that Jason and I reconnected and decided to go out on a date.

I realized there would be challenges in dating Jason. I love his parents. We all laugh a bit looking back at my first visit to their house. Let's just say it was a little less than ideal. In fact, I didn't even make it inside the house. I only made it to the front porch. It was clear that there was some reluctance to the idea of Jason dating me. At that time there weren't a whole lot of mixed-race couples running around their neighborhood.

When dating it became obvious to Jason and me that we would face challenges—not just from family, but from many others. It was also in the process of dating that I saw that Jason was an all in, committed person. I was his girl, and he was my man, and he wasn't ever going to allow anything or anyone to get between us. It is easy for people to say they are all in. It is another thing to live all in. Jason has been living all in every day of our marriage and journey together.

Four months after our first date, we were married. Although we were certain that we would face significant, unique challenges as a biracial couple, we committed to one another for time and all eternity. Our belief that marriage and family extend into the eternities has strengthened our commitment to each other in the here and now and provided a long-term perspective that helps during difficult days or trying times.

Jason has been my partner and greatest support system throughout this journey. Recently on the *Studio 5* program on KSL-TV, host Brooke Walker did a Valentine's Day look at some political couples. Brooke recognized that each couple, from John and Abigail Adams to

Eleanor and Franklin Roosevelt, had a superpower that kept their relationship strong and dynamic. Jason and I were featured as one of the couples. I loved that they chose for our superpower: "All in, all the time!"

Here is how they described the way we deployed the "all in, all the time" superpower:

> I have watched this duo support each other for a number of years. They are really amazing and whether it is Mia creating space for Jason to do what he does best in his work and career or Jason rearranging things so Mia could serve in government and raise her voice—they are so all in.
>
> The morning Mia was sworn in as the first Black Republican Woman in Congress they went for a run on the national mall—together—side-by-side as always. It was symbolic of how they got there and what they would continue [to] do in the years ahead. For the Loves [their dynamic relationship] isn't about a division of labor or being a supportive spouse—it is way beyond that—it is all in.[1]

I am very thankful for the little things that brought Jason and me together, and ultimately our amazing children into our family. So many hinge points.

Another of those early hinges that began turning my

political wheels was actually Jason's father. As a long-time Republican, Jason's dad had a great influence on the conservative values and ideals I would come to know, apply, and eventually promote.

As a lifelong learner, I was always open to new ideas, and I found discussing current world issues to be most interesting when I would visit my father-in-law. We would talk for hours about policy and current events. We would go back and forth sharing our individual takes on issues, events, and opportunities in the community and nation.

As I dug deeper into principles, policies, and politics with Jason's family, I realized most of my core beliefs and values actually aligned with the Republican Party. This was a "wow" moment for me!

Growing up I knew most of my Black friends were Democrats. They often referred to the Republican Party as not being tolerant of, or even being against, minority communities. I recognized that there were some past members of the Republican Party who fit that description. I also understood that the party's principles and policies were not owned, nor best exemplified, by any one particular politician. While the GOP is often referred to as the party of Abraham Lincoln, I was certain that Lincoln would not condone, and would rightly condemn, the actions of those who failed to live up to the principles they professed to believe.

Thankfully, I had learned from my father-in-law

the critical need to focus on the principles and policies rather than the personalities of specific politicians. That hinge became vital for me over the years as I interacted with party leaders and politicians from both sides of the aisle. This little "midge" of learning always allowed me to speak honestly and openly with anyone, anywhere, anytime. Gaining the confidence to speak truth to power can be realized only when you have built a foundation of principles.

I learned that speaking truth to power—including years later when speaking it to the occupant of the highest office in the land—is not always easy and can be politically costly. I am thankful I had these early conversations with Jason's dad as they gave me the confidence to do and say the right things, regardless of the consequences or which powerful person was in the room.

I learned that the Republican Party was established to hold certain standards, pursue certain issues, and implement certain policies for the good of the people. Principles like smaller government, personal responsibility, free markets, and federalism (that most of the power is allocated to the states and to the people, and that government closest to the people governs best) all resonated with me. I recognized that I personally believed in and would absolutely stand for so many of those principles and the policies they produced for the people.

I believe in a decentralized government, a free market

economy, and the unalienable rights of the people to live by the dictates of their own consciences.

I could see that Washington had been ruining America rather than repairing it. For decades America had been running into all of the big problems that big government brings. I came to believe that it is *not* okay to have a government that lies to you and spies on you and then targets those who oppose its agenda. In other words, I knew America required transparency and free speech and that agencies can become too powerful and use a number of ways to spy on citizens before targeting them through taxes, regulation, and mandates.

I recognized the enormous problems that stem from presidents of either political party believing they are all powerful and are willing to rule through executive orders rather than Congress. A president's actions—as President Barack Obama popularized—with a cell phone and a pen damage the economy as well as our communities. To be clear, President Obama was neither the first nor the last to do extensive damage through executive orders.

My personal philosophy began to be galvanized with the idea that when government grows, freedom shrinks, and once a freedom is taken away, it is rarely—if ever—given back.

In America our lives should not be driven by government dictates but by individual dreams. I would often tell audiences of all kinds that I knew they had dreams for themselves and for their children. And I am certain they didn't pick up those dreams standing in line at the DMV or find them on some government website.

I truly believe that American dreams are a cottage industry—fostered at home, built with our hands, nurtured in our hearts—where even the National Security Agency (NSA) can't intrude.

Through my parents' teachings and new insights gained from Jason's father, I came to passionately believe for myself that the solutions to our problems don't come from looking to Washington; they are found when we look within.

Another hinge that turned and shaped my philosophy was watching how things were done in Utah. There is this thing we like to call the "Utah Model." It is based in a free market economy and is fueled by a fiscally responsible limited government with a light regulatory system that empowers entrepreneurs.

Utah also has robust institutions of civil society with social capital that makes Utah one of the most upwardly mobile places on earth. (Meaning someone born into poverty, or who falls into poverty, has a better chance of getting out of poverty and achieving upward mobility than anywhere else in America.) The best way to protect and elevate those in poverty is by giving them an avenue to rise and succeed through their own labor and the effort they are willing to exert.

Finally, Utah, while being a very red political state, has also shown that you can reject the fake fights and false political choices of Washington. Utah has led the way toward real, compassionate immigration reform as well as proving that LGBTQ rights and religious liberty are compatible.

So rather than focusing on what happens in DC boardrooms and backrooms, I have been able to focus on what is happening in living rooms and especially at kitchen tables across America.

Big government doesn't work! It is when hard-working Americans apply these principles that our communities work. I have become convinced that we are not one Harvard graduate or one charismatic politician away from prosperity, or one government program away from solving our nation's deepest problems.

Government clearly has a role in helping create space for liberty, justice, and the equal opportunity to the pursuit of happiness. I have come to believe that conservative principles have lifted *more* people out of poverty, fueled *more* freedom, and driven *more* dreams than any other set of principles in the history of the world.

In Washington we don't need more mercenaries; we need better messengers—people who not only talk about conservative principles but boldly apply them!

Conservative principles and conservative policies work; I have *seen* them work as a mayor and as a mother.

I do believe that it takes a village; we just have to remember that the village is *not* the government. The village is you and me working together for our families and communities.

The principles I discussed with my father-in-law during our many conversations simply rang true in my heart. I believe they rang true because my parents had sounded them in my soul as a young girl. My love for my country and my belief that America is a land of promise, brimming with hopes and dreams, has strengthened, inspired, and blessed me throughout my life.

My parents had proven that the principles of America work. They showed me that the content of your character matters and is ultimately what qualifies you to rise and succeed. I have lived the blessings of liberty they secured for me and my posterity.

These American principles solidified a firm foundation that was wide and deep enough for me to be open, to explore every idea, every possibility, and every policy position—regardless of which political party or member of Congress proposed it. I have learned that my voice is stronger, smarter, and more powerfully sincere after I listen to others—especially those I disagree with.

After a season of listening and exploring the issues impacting the world around me, I began to formulate my personal principles and policy preferences. I adopted many conservative ideals, but I never believed everything was right with the Republican Party. I don't believe political parties own principles or even policies. Principles before political party has always been my guidepost. Sticking to that in an age of cynicism and political extremism hasn't always been easy. But it has always been worth it.

I was appalled when midges covered the walls of our house, our windows, and our doors when we moved into our home in Saratoga Springs. These pesky pests were everywhere and threatened the excitement and joy of our first home in what we believed was a wonderful neighborhood. It didn't take long for me to recognize that my house was not the only one suffering under the tiny, yet unrelenting annoyance of the swarming midges. A group of frustrated and beleaguered homeowners petitioned for the builder to follow common practice and treat our community with a spray that would control the midges. The builder refused.

Jokingly, I threw out the idea to the other new moms of the community that we might be able to convince the builder to treat the midges if we put signs in our yards warning prospective homebuyers to stay away.

The idea quickly went from idea to action, and the Mom Squad staked handwritten warning signs in front of our homes saying DON'T BUY A HOUSE HERE! and SAVE

YOURSELF FROM THE MIDGES! and WE REGRET BUYING A HOUSE HERE! These signs raised our voices and our concerns.

Amazingly, our raised voices were heard. Within just a few weeks, the builder came to us to offer a compromise. The builder would treat the midges in exchange for our agreeing to remove the signs from our front yards.

The doors of my political history turned on that little effort to eliminate those tiny midges.

This very modest and simple grassroots victory inspired me as a leader with the Mom Squad to pursue a role on the city council. Our neighborhood had no representation on the current council, and our town was growing at a breathtaking rate. We realized we had a voice and that our community needed a voice on the city council.

Those pesky midges had turned a hinge in my heart and unlocked a part of me. I suddenly recognized I could be part of the solution to problems and challenges facing my friends, neighbors, and community. It was as though those midges had tapped into something I had felt as a performer on the stage and in the color guard. Feelings of being part of something bigger than myself, to be a player on a stage that mattered and could make a difference.

My vision was expanded in ways I couldn't have imagined. My desire to serve grew. I confess that the idea of serving in political positions never really had resonated with me. I think this was because up to this point I had viewed politicians with skepticism and a sense that many were in it just for themselves and for their own power and popularity. But through the midges I came to realize that most who enter the fray of politics do so because they are compelled or propelled by an experience, like mine, with a midge-type problem that they were passionate about solving. Having done it once, the prospects of solving other problems or improving conditions and impacting a community becomes incredibly compelling.

While my problem-solving passion had been ignited by the midges, I was still very uncertain that I was actually qualified to hold an elected office.

With the encouragement of the ever-positive Mom Squad and the support of my husband, Jason, I put my name on the ballot for city council. My first campaign was nothing spectacular, but I did what I do best—raised my voice and talked to people, and then listened to what they had to say.

Through knocking on doors, I learned about my neighbors' concerns, wants, and needs. Conscious of what my ethnicity might mean or suggest to the predominantly white community, I put little elephants on my signs to be posted around town to demonstrate my credibility. Those tiny elephants might have been what gave me enough confidence that I was actually qualified for the role and belonged on the ballot.

After a third-place result in the primary, I was in the race. There were three empty city council seats; I just needed one of them. Through sharing my story and raising my voice, I began to slowly and subtly recognize that the content of my character qualified me to serve my neighbors. I pushed forward toward the general election—on the hinges of midges.

That first election night taught me lessons for future election nights: It is never over until it is over, there are always surprises, and winning is always more fun than losing. On that first election night, we were surprised and overjoyed to realize that I was not only one of the three winners, but I had managed to pull in more votes than any of my competitors.

You always remember the first. As a family we were pleased and proud. Our pride, however, paled in comparison to the pride of my parents. My accomplishment was the fulfillment of what my father said to me when he dropped me off at college years before: "You will give back." This campaign victory for a city council seat was my first introduction into a role that would teach me the importance of political representation and shape my view of the proper role of government for years to come.

The door for my political future swung open the night

of that election. Looking back, however, it is easy for me to see that the hinges to my political path actually started to turn long before those midges came along and well before I took a flying leap into the city council race.

Tiny hinges—yes, the size of midges—have swung open doors of opportunity and gates of understanding throughout my life and career.

CHAPTER 5

Running to, Not Away

There were many instances during my time in Congress when I felt the urge to run away. Sometimes it was running away from a reporter who was determined to corner me with bad questions, bad intentions, and with their prewritten bad story—regardless of my answers. Other times it was running away from my own political party leadership members who were trying to convince me that casting a bad vote would be good for my reelection prospects. Sometimes it was running away from the circus that is Washington, DC, or the rat race of perpetual fund-raising for colleagues or the party.

More running.

I had learned early in my political career that running away was never the answer. It was what you were running for and what you were running to that mattered.

In 2009, when I was a city council member, the mayor of Saratoga Springs announced he would not seek reelection. The council was in the midst of tireless work trying to pull our city from the grips of financial meltdown and potential ruin. More troubling to me than the mayor stepping down were the local characters who announced they were going to mount campaigns to take the mayorship for themselves. None would have fit my definition of "statesman" or "servant of the people." There were many with personal agendas and big political aspirations.

As our city was frantically looking for a respectable candidate, several of my city council members confronted me and asked me to consider running for mayor. That was a "run away" moment for me. They were asking me to run for the good of the city and toward a brighter future for the expanding number of citizens coming to the area. They wanted me to run toward the need to continue putting the city's financial house back on solid ground and preparing for additional growth and opportunity.

Running away from that moment would have been easy. I had done some good work, had sacrificed, and would have been justified in thinking that perhaps I had done enough.

Although I looked for a way out or a reason to run

to something other than the mayor's race, my father's words came back to me in this moment, as they have many times since.

My mind ran back to my father's solemn look on that first day on campus at Hartford when he told me that he and my mom had done everything they could to get me to where I was. That they had never taken a thing from the government, and that I was not to be a burden to society. I still hear his final words, "You will give back."

This led me to do things I never expected to do. It has always led me to run toward things and for things that matter—and not just in politics.

On that day, almost incredulously, I walked myself to the registrar at City Hall and submitted my name for the mayoral candidacy. It seemed surreal. I had no idea how to really run this kind of race. It was going to be a different kind of race, with a different kind of running than is typical of most mayoral races.

The questions of "Who do you think you are?" and "You can't possibly think you are qualified for this position, can you?" echoed in my head. I was actually pretty sure I wasn't qualified to be a mayor, especially as I reflected on other mayoral races around the country.

Just for comparison, to win the mayor's race in New York City in 2009, Mayor Michael Bloomberg spent $109 million of his own money. At the time, about 8 million people called New York City home. Bloomberg doled out

$14,000 for every single human in his city to claim his third term in office.[1] I began my mayoral campaign with two donors who supported me and generously contributed $1,500 for my budget, which equated to less than a dime per person of the population of Saratoga Springs.

The majority of my campaign was spent doing what I do best—running and talking to *everyone*.

And I knew the little-known secret about Utah politics: Even with all the white males dominating the state's elected offices, it's the women of Utah who are the kingmakers, movers, shakers, and difference makers. It's a dangerous thing to overlook the power of a woman.

I was introduced to a string of powerful and connected women who provided their counsel to me during my campaign. We dubbed the group the "Yacht Club." The hidden analogy of the Yacht Club was women making waves.

This tribe of sisters became a lifeline in so many ways. They were also a power line to the elevated principles, policies, and strategies I desperately needed. I still can't imagine a world in politics without them. They have always had my back and have been supportive to the end.

The Yacht Club included Deidre Henderson (who is now the lieutenant governor of Utah), Holly Richardson, Heather Groom, Mandee Grant, Sarah Nitta, Dr. DeLaina Tonks, Adrielle Herring, and Heather Jackson.

These women not only had my back from the very start but, more important, they validated me and helped me overcome my own insecurities. We often met at lunch to discuss the state of politics, public debates, and campaigns. We have laughed and cried together and mourned together. We have agreed and disagreed and come to appreciate each other in deep ways.

Over the years the ladies of the Yacht Club have made a lot of waves in Utah. For me personally, they have always been there to defend me against political sharks and help me navigate rough water. At times they have unleashed holy hell on political opportunists and rallied communities and campaign volunteers to support me.

My only regret was not realizing how much they were willing to help. I've always had trouble asking for help when I really needed it. That imposter syndrome had me, and so many others, too afraid to ask for help, admit weaknesses, or show vulnerability.

It is important for everyone to understand what imposter syndrome is, since I know I am not the only one who has experienced it. I actually believe that imposter syndrome is what keeps many women and minorities from running for office or leaning into leadership opportunities in their careers and communities.

"Imposter syndrome" is the antithesis of "qualified." Rather than your feeling qualified by the content of your character, imposter syndrome leads you to self-doubt, self-sabotage, and a complete undermining of self-esteem. You become worried about people discovering that your life isn't perfect, that you don't have the answer to everything, and that you have a list of habits that need improvement. Imposter syndrome leads you to live in a position of weakness or in a defensive crouch, waiting for the other shoe to drop or for people to realize that you really don't belong.

Some pretty accomplished people share that feeling of imposter syndrome. Poet Maya Angelou said, "I have written 11 books but each time I think, 'Uh oh, they're going to find out now. I've run a game on everybody, and they're going to *find me out*'"[2] [emphasis added].

U.S. Supreme Court Justice Sonia Sotomayor has commented on a number of occasions about wondering if she belonged while on the campus at Princeton. One description of her memoir stated, "She puts us in the Harvard/ Radcliffe admissions office circa 1970, where everything from the oriental rug to the white couch to the perfectly coiffed hair of the admissions officer conspire to say: you don't belong here if you're from the Bronx."[3]

"You don't belong" can be a devastating, disheartening, and isolating echo in your mind.

Albert Einstein once said, "The exaggerated esteem in which my lifework is held makes me very ill at ease. I feel compelled to think of myself as an involuntary swindler."[4]

Actress Emma Watson put it this way: "It's almost like the better I do, the more my feeling of inadequacy actually increases, because I'm just going, *Any moment, someone's going to find out I'm a total fraud, and that I don't deserve any of what I've achieved.*"[5]

I know you aren't reading my book as a self-help or motivational exercise. But I want to include something from Dr. Valerie Young as way to help you overcome imposter syndrome and embrace your "qualified" self!

Young divided imposter syndrome into five categories:

1. The Perfectionist: You set excessively high goals for yourself, then beat yourself up if you're not perfect 100 percent of the time.
2. Superwoman/-man: Convinced you are a phony when everyone else is the real deal, so do more, more, more to prove you measure up.
3. The Natural Genius: Things normally come easy, so if you are unable to do something perfectly the first time, you wonder what is wrong with you.
4. The Rugged Individualist: You believe that if you ask for help, it proves you are incapable.
5. The Expert: Somehow feel you have tricked your employer into hiring you; you constantly seek additional training and certifications to prove you know your stuff, but you never feel like you know enough.[6]

In the midst of running my campaign, I realized that I wasn't the only woman or minority who regularly had feelings of being an imposter. I had come to understand that I had spent too much time running away from feeling inadequate and not enough time running toward my strengths, skills, and natural gifts. My Yacht Club friends, and later the women of the Congressional Black Caucus, helped me reject imposter syndrome and fully embrace a more qualified approach to life.

I also discovered during this mayoral race the challenge many women face in running for office—and even why some women have difficulty voting for women: I was struck at one point when a woman I spoke with during my campaign informed me regretfully that she couldn't vote for me because she had just grown up believing that men do a better job in this type of political position.

I realized at that point that I was running against some attitudes, beliefs, and biases that would make my race challenging. I learned that I couldn't run against those things. I had to simply set such arguments aside and demonstrate what I was running for.

I was going door to door talking with local citizens when I came to an older man who was mowing his lawn. He asked me a question that I hadn't quite asked or answered for myself in the context of a political race. "What is the role of government?"

He told me to find my answer before I was bold enough to seek a real position of power. It was good advice. This led me, during my campaign and throughout my career, to study political thinkers of all stripes and to begin shaping my own political doctrine.

At that moment in that mayoral campaign, it caused me to go back and reflect on the many conversations I had had with Jason and his dad. Suddenly, I realized all those fun, entertaining, and illuminating chats were no longer chin-stroking ruminations or political navel-gazing; they were about to become very real for me and would make a profound difference in the way I would lead and the results I would achieve in elected office.

Understanding the proper role of government would lead me to understand what I was running and fighting for in an elected office, rather than just what I was running against.

The role of government, I came to believe, is to protect individual liberties. Elected leaders are tasked with ensuring that power stays with the people. The people are the keepers of the Constitution, and the people are to remain vigilant in holding their elected officials accountable to the laws of the land. Both jobs are equally vital to the health of the country.

While understanding what I was running for, I developed a series of questions that have become my touchstone when faced with policy questions or spending decisions:

1. Is this policy affordable?
2. Is this program sustainable?
3. Is implementing or funding this my job?

I then knew what I was running for and what I wanted to lead our city toward.

So many bright spotlights are turned to the players in Washington, DC, but the real hard work, heavy lifting, and big impact happen on the field at the local level. I learned from my parents that looking to Washington to solve problems is not the path to better days. You have to look within—within each individual and each community. This reinforced my desire to share with voters my vision for what we could do—together.

My opponents seemed more focused on a vision of themselves in office than a vision for the people of the community. Because my opponents had failed to share and demonstrate what they were truly running for, I entered election night confident.

I want to note here three leadership lessons that I realized in the midst of my first mayor's race that guided me in every campaign. I actually use these lessons to inform my thinking when I choose who to vote for in every election.

First, when you begin to assess a candidate that you are considering, see where their words and actions take you. When you listen to this candidate, where do those words lead your thoughts? It really isn't so much what a candidate says as it is where those words take you. When you listen to the candidate, do you find yourself thinking just about the candidate and their story, or do you find yourself thinking about your life, family, or future? Do your thoughts go toward feelings of fear, frustration, and conflict, or toward positive solutions and possibilities? A candidate whose words lead your thinking to negative places or solely into the candidate's world is not the one to lead you, your city, or the country toward a better, brighter future.

Second, what is this candidate running for? You know what the candidate is against—starting with their competitors for the nomination and the opposing party. While the candidate has to be willing to fight against the kind of government they don't want, they must also be able to articulate the kind of government they do want. Do they have an agenda they can point to that expresses in principles and by policies what kind of government, community, or country they intend to foster?

Third, is this candidate more interested in making friends, getting likes on social media, and making news, or are they committed to keeping promises? Many politicians have become way too eager to get along, go along, and make deals that are good for them but not necessarily good for their constituents. Real friends tell you the truth; even when it is hard, they tell you what needs to be done to solve your problems without sugar-coating it and demonstrate to you by their actions that they will stand with you no matter what.

I ran this first mayoral race all the way to the end. I tried to make the three questions above part of who I was and part of every conversation I had with potential voters. I began to own who I was as a person, as a member of the community, and potentially as the mayor of this rapidly growing city faced with significant financial challenges.

Coming down the homestretch, I began to take heart in the confidence friends and neighbors had in me. It amazed me then, and continued to surprise me through every campaign, what citizens are willing to do to achieve what they believe will benefit their community and country. Hours of knocking on doors, putting up signs, dialing voters, running campaign events, organizing get-out-the-vote efforts—people do extraordinary things and really are willing to do hard things. I was especially amazed that people would do all of this even when the outcome was uncertain—just for the chance of being part of something special. We ran until the very second the polls closed.

As the votes began to come in on election night, it was clear that the people had spoken and that what I was running for was what voters were voting for. It was a great night and an important win for me. Yet, perhaps my biggest victory of the night was when I saw my new friend, the woman who had said she couldn't vote for a woman and who had sworn to her traditional beliefs. She said, "Mia, it's all you. I'm putting my faith in you. I need you to prove me right!"

On election night, we were at Avondale Academy, a little elementary school. When the results became official, I said to my son Peyton, "Guess what? I'm the mayor!"

Peyton burst out, "I won!" There was a guy from the *Salt Lake Tribune* taking pictures there, and Peyton was running around shouting, "I did it! I did it!" He had been with me all the way and even done some of the work—and yes, he thought he won. "I won, Dad!" he said. "Did you hear? I'm the mayor. I won!" He then asked if he was going to get paid real money for being the mayor!

Not long after I won the election, Peyton, who has no filter, started to say to everybody and anybody who would listen, "Hey, do you know my mom? She's Mia Love. She won! You should say hi to her." We were at the Ross department store, and Peyton was running around telling everyone who I was and that they should come over to meet me. I finally took him out of Ross because it was getting kind of embarrassing and a little out of hand. Fast-forward a few days, and it was starting to go to little Peyton's head. He started to say, "I am Peyton Love. Do you know me? My mom's Mia Love. Remember when I won the election?" A little zeal without knowledge, but I loved his enthusiasm and that he felt that he was part of it all.

I take my kids everywhere because they're part of me. I want them to see me working hard and what that kind of work can produce. I also want them to see what service looks like. It's not sitting on your butt. I remember taking my kids on every campaign—the congressional campaign, the mayoral campaign. During those early elections it was Peyton in a stroller, Abi handing out flyers, and Alessa handing out flyers while saying, "Hey, would you like to talk to my mom? She's over here. We can stop by your house later if you're busy. Don't worry, she won't stop by your house and bother you—you should just get to know her." Campaigning taught my children to be respectful, even with those who disagreed with them. They also learned not to be shy. My kids learned many lessons because of my service—including the value of trust.

Given my "unicorn status" in Utah as a Black female Republican, I knew that people occasionally would have to muster up their faith and go against what they had always believed in order to cast their vote for me. From this very first mayoral race, I have felt deeply and carried with me the personal responsibility of every vote. I feel the sacredness of that trust, and I honor the time it takes for someone to become educated on issues and candidates, then make the effort to enter a voting booth and click on my name or sit at their kitchen table and mark the ballot on my behalf.

Trust is the hardest thing to earn and the easiest thing to lose. I never wanted to do anything that would cause any voter or constituent to question the trust they had placed in me. Even now, I can look in the eye every person who voted for me for any office and know there's nothing I've done that would make them ashamed for putting their faith in me. That is the handshake agreement every voter should have with every elected official.

Our communities and country desperately need more women and minorities who are willing to raise their voices on crucial conversations and step into local political races. Even against odds and adversity, success is possible with determination, staying true to who you are, and having a vision of where you want to go. Never underestimate the influence you can have.

Don't get caught comparing your weaknesses with other people's strengths. Don't question whether or not you belong. Don't worry about being a political novice. Don't worry if those you run against have bigger names or bank accounts. Don't worry if occasionally you even feel a little bit of imposter syndrome.

Focus on your vision of what you are for and invite

people to join you in the journey toward something better. With confidence, intelligence, and strategy, you can successfully make a political or professional advance.

You can run for something. You don't need a million-dollar budget; you simply need to know that you are qualified by the content of your character. Above all, know that you can win!

CHAPTER 6

Bounce-ability and Making History

G eneral George Patton reportedly said, "The test of success is not what you do when you are on top. Success is how high you bounce when you hit bottom."[1]

I was on a pretty good run from city council to mayor and into the race for Utah's Fourth Congressional District. As I noted earlier, the path to the Republican nomination was fraught with challenges of many kinds. But I did have a few things in my favor that were important.

I mentioned that the Republican delegates had moved further right during the previous election cycle. Well, in the 2012 cycle, Republican senator Orrin Hatch was up for reelection and was determined that he wouldn't end up with the same kind of loss that Bob Bennett had suffered in 2010. Senator Hatch knew that if the slate of delegates was similar to 2010, he would lose for sure. He spent an enormous amount of money to get delegates more favorable to him elected to represent their local precincts. That turned out to be very beneficial for me, given that my opponents were already well-known among the 2010 delegates.

Just prior to the convention I was told, once again, to just wait my turn. I was literally told that I wasn't experienced enough, that I was not qualified—even though I had served on the city council and as mayor, and my city was really successful. Saratoga Springs was an up-and-coming community, and it was actually named one of the top cities for growth and financial success.

There were other little miracles that came together, like the "I'm a Mormon" video on the Church of Jesus Christ website that Janna Ryan had seen and sent to her husband, Paul. And true to her pronouncement, she got Paul Ryan to help this lady from Utah on the video.

Having made it through the convention to secure the Republican nomination, we were now facing the big battle ahead in November.

Jim Matheson, a six-term Democratic Second District incumbent, announced that he would run for the Fourth Congressional District position as the Democratic candidate. His decision to run in the newly created Fourth District was big news and a big challenge for my campaign. The new Fourth Congressional District had Saratoga Springs right in the middle of it. Jim actually found out that his house was outside of the district, but he still believed it was his best chance for reelection.

The race was a continuous experience in the "school of hard knocks." The campaign was brutal, and the attacks were personal. National groups spent tons of money both against and for me. Often when it seemed like we were getting our footing, another attack or small failure of execution seemed to knock us back down.

Some nights I dreamed I was forever pushing the rock up the hill, only to get to the top and have it roll right back down to the bottom. I felt like the campaign had become like Sisyphus, who was punished by the god Zeus. Sisyphus was forced to roll a boulder up a hill for eternity, and every time he got to the top of the hill, the boulder would roll back down to the valley floor. Some mornings it was challenging to face that campaign rock and the mountain I needed to roll it up.

After enduring the bumps, bruises, and lessons of a knock-down, drag-out campaign, the first Tuesday of November finally came. We finally made it to election night. We were at the Hilton Hotel. We were with family, friends, politicians, and volunteers from all the Republican campaigns. It was simply a crazy night. We had our war room with the pollsters, trackers, and the campaign team.

Everyone was watching the results come in. We also spent some time watching the national news, which had Mitt Romney losing a tough race against President Barack Obama. That had a little dampening effect on the night.

Despite the fact that we were actually feeling good about our prospects of winning, no one on our team had any real experience running this kind of campaign. None of us did. We didn't quite understand what to do when the Matheson team called Steve Hunter, a supporter and member of the campaign team, to get my phone number.

Matheson's team wanted my phone number because they anticipated his loss as the results coming in actually had us winning. I was convinced that the night was going to be historic for us.

But by two o'clock in the morning, the clarity of the numbers had dwindled, confusion had begun to settle in, and we didn't know anything. Sadly, those hours drifted into days and extended to weeks. It wasn't until close to the end of November that we finally knew the final results, which came when Salt Lake County got around to releasing its completed canvass.

As those weeks had dragged on, our family decided the best thing to do was to take a quick decompression vacation to Disneyland. That's right—I was in the Magic Kingdom when the pixie dust of our campaign finally ran out. There was no happily ever after for the 2012 campaign. No fireworks closing the scene, no fade to black as the credits rolled.

We lost. That was an incredibly difficult thing to process. To work so hard, to see so many miraculous things come together and then lose in the end. The mental gymnastics were exhausting. Jim handed me my first major loss in the political realm by a grand total of 768 votes in a three-way election. I had so many what-if questions—and a very large question mark of where to go from here and what to do next.

I am no fan of losing. The entire family took the loss very hard. My disappointment was compounded by the sense that my children and husband and friends and extended family had invested so much time, emotion, and energy into the race; I worried that I had let them all down. My competitiveness keeps me wanting to win. But in losing this race, I had the opportunity to learn some lessons in bounce-ability and perspective. One of the first calls I received after my loss was declared final was from Arizona senator John McCain. He had been helpful to me during my race, and in his classic maverick kind of way he said, "Mia, this race was an investment in your future. You will run again, and you will win."

I did not let this loss slow me down or silence my voice. Unleashed from any other agenda or organization, I was free to speak the ideals and values of my heart.

I learned that your voice doesn't go away when your platform does. At least it shouldn't. The defeat motivated me to ramp up my understanding of policy, hone the message around the principles that I hold dear, and work to connect even better to the people I wanted to represent.

I tried to not let the loss undercut my confidence. I knew I was qualified. The campaign had taught me to own my story—in an authentic, unapologetic way. I had found my voice in significant speeches during the campaign and in conversations with people in my district. I had galvanized my confidence that I could lead, and ultimately be judged by the content of my character, and I recognized that I could empower and inspire others to join an important cause.

Trying to get the maximum benefit of bouncing off the bottom of a political defeat, I determined that I needed some zen activities in my life.

Campaigns are exhausting, to say the least—win or lose—but especially in losing. I decided I wanted to learn to paint with oils as a new hobby and semidistraction. Per usual, Jason was patient and absolutely supportive of my pursuit. He waited and waited at the store as I purchased all the paints, easels, brushes, and canvasses I thought I needed. Of course, what I thought I needed and what I actually needed were two very different things, but Jason indulged it all and expressed confidence that this was going to be a good thing for me to jump into following the tough political defeat.

With all the tools and materials that I could possibly need, I began to paint. I really knew nothing about painting, especially with oil. Within just minutes I found that I was painting Mount Timpanogos in Utah. It was a mountain I looked up at every day. I was familiar with it, and I had hiked in, on, and around it. I could see it when I went on my morning run or when I was taking my kids to school. When I finished, I was really proud of my work. Painting wasn't really that difficult after all. Or so I thought.

With great confidence I began my second painting. This was going to be a beautiful English countryside. I worked and worked and worked on it. I began to get incredibly frustrated because every countryside I attempted to paint looked like Mount Timpanogos in the end!

I realized that I had never been to the English countryside and didn't really know what it looked like. I went online and scoured all kinds of pictures from England. The vegetation was vastly different from Mount Timpanogos. Everything was different, actually.

I learned that you can't paint what you don't know. People only know what they know, and if they aren't willing to learn from others, they can only paint where they have been or what they have seen in their limited experience. This gave me an incredible bounce as I considered the possibility of my second congressional run. I didn't want to paint another Timpanogos campaign based on what I had already seen and done.

I also learned in this in-between period following my defeat that failure does not disqualify you from using your voice. Instead, I discovered that failure can be used as a catalyst for greater focus, determination, and planning new adventures.

Make no mistake, the loss stung. There were moments when I wondered if all the effort, hassle, headache, and heartache were worth it. Having lost such a tight race, I found that you could spend a lot of time in the "would have, could have, should have" department. I quickly recognized that was no place for me. That is the test of any setback. I had learned that the only thing I could control was my bounce-ability; it was my determination to learn from the past and prepare for the future that mattered most.

The content of your character is not determined or defined by past failures. Character is found in that bounce-ability that propels you toward the future. Both Jason and I were feeling some bounce to run a second time.

Having experienced the sting of defeat in November 2012, we had to ask questions about whether we really wanted to go through all that again, about what if we ran and lost again and whether or not we really had it in us to go for it in 2014. Jason told me, "Mia, call Dave Hansen. He knows how to do this. If Dave thinks that we have a chance of winning, then we should ask him to run the campaign."

Now, Dave had run many successful campaigns in Utah and had just run a successful campaign for Senator Hatch. He knew the lay of the land in Utah politics and where the bodies were buried, and he understood how to win.

So we met with Dave at the Kneaders restaurant in Saratoga Springs. Jason and I asked him a ton of questions, including what he thought our chances of winning would be. Dave said we had a solid 60 percent chance of winning. He said that this district was still new for Jim and that it was going to be a difficult race no matter what. Dave was encouraging, because he recognized that I had learned how to raise both local and national money.

We called Dave on New Year's Eve and asked if he would be willing to meet us for breakfast the next morning. Yes—New Year's Day 2013. We asked him, "Will you run this campaign?" Dave said, "Yes, I think it would be fun!"

Dave began to put the pieces of the campaign together. He knew what to do. He definitely knew what to do. We asked what the first thing we needed to do to change the outcome this time around was. Without hesitation he said, "You have to outraise Matheson. Every. Single. Quarter!" And we did!

I determined that I would get my policy ideas from the people who had been places I hadn't. My veterans' policies came from actual veterans who had dealt with physical and emotional trauma and struggled to get what they needed from the VA and other agencies. Policies for senior citizens actually came from the time I spent in senior living centers listening to the experiences from the greatest generation about what it was like to navigate Social Security, Medicare—trying to get the prescription medicines they needed—and other programs. My education policy came from talking to parents, teachers, and administrators who were living it all every single day.

I continued to have crucial conversations with key constituents. We kept outraising Matheson. We felt good about where we were and the progress we were making. We knew that we had the money to run the campaign that we needed to run, and we had Dave calling the shots.

Even under the best of circumstances, campaigns are long, grueling, and mentally exhausting. For Jason and me that also included balancing his work, all the kids' activities, and more. Some days on the campaign trail you just wonder if it is worth all the sacrifice of time, emotional energy, and stress.

Jason wrote in his journal about a very pivotal moment in our journey. He recorded his concerns and worries and the prayers he had been offering. Jason needed some divine guidance as he tried to wrap his head around the last campaign while plunging headlong into the next one. Jason worried that even though things had come together, miracles had happened, and many people had been inspired, in the end nothing had happened. We had lost.

Jason prayed fervently that he was willing to sacrifice, to run the gambit of campaign life again, and ultimately give up his wife for long stretches of time so she could go and serve. Then Jason asked the bigger question—it was the other side of the prayer I had offered in the bathroom stall at the convention site in Tampa. Jason basically put it this way: "Lord, if it's not for your purpose, or for your will to be done, then tell me this is not what we're supposed to do."

It was that profound. And he read that journal entry to me one night. He prayed specifically, "Help me understand if this is what we're supposed to do. And if it is what we are supposed to do, please speak in a language which I can understand. Please!"

In December 2013, I was out at the grocery store doing some quick shopping. While I was casually rolling my cart down the aisle, my phone rang. I can't even remember who it was that called me, but I will forever remember what they said: "Matheson just dropped out of the race."

I was a little incredulous and asked why in the world he would do that. They said, "Check it out, it's all over Facebook." Right in the middle of the cereal section of the store, my phone started just ringing off the hook. Of course, I didn't answer any of the calls.

I called Jason. We had just had the conversation, and Jason had read me his journal entry. I immediately repeated to Jason, "Did you ask in your prayer that God would speak in a way that was clear that we could understand?"

Jason repeated back, "I said, 'Lord, we're spending a lot of time on this. And if we should invest our efforts in other ways to serve, we would really appreciate you letting us know. Because this is challenging, and we just don't have any clarity in the right path forward.'" Well, Jim's dropping out of the race was a pretty clear way for us to understand there was a path to victory and service!

I soon got a phone call from Paul Ryan. He said, "Mia, we know exactly what this is. Jim won't say it. But we know what this is. He was going to lose and would rather go off on his own terms than to lose a race. So he retired. Jim does have a consulting opportunity, and that is great. And you now have an opportunity, so get after it."

And so that was what we did.

Interestingly, the moment Jim bowed out, all of a

sudden there were a number of Republicans interested in jumping into the race. There were some opportunists who saw it as their big chance to not have to face Jim Matheson as an incumbent. The only potential challenger that was a little troubling to me was the husband of our treasurer for the campaign. But those threats came and went pretty swiftly.

Jim's announcement that he would not be running for reelection was a major surprise to many. I instantly became the favored candidate.

On April 26, 2014, I won the Republican nomination for the Fourth Congressional District at the Utah Republican Convention with 78 percent of the vote. I would be up against Doug Owens, the Democratic Party nominee, in the general election.

My experience in bounce-ability, which I gained in defeat, helped me navigate the race with Owens in a way that was more comfortable, more confident, and more consistent with the principles I held, my personal story, and the vision I had of the future.

On election day, I gained the lead as the final votes were counted that evening, and eventually pulled ahead by more than seven thousand votes.

Bounce-ability turned into history. I became the first Black Republican congresswoman.

I ran on values like the need for increased grass-roots organization within the GOP. I focused on smaller government and bigger citizens and the need for independence from the government.

With a national platform, much of it built during my failed campaign in 2012, I now had a position in Congress. I knew my influence had expanded. I recognized I had been elected for a reason and put in a position to use my voice for the greater good. People had put their trust in me and given me more opportunity and responsibility. I recognized the weight of this role and wanted to make my parents, my own husband and children, and my constituents proud.

Bounce-ability gives you the resilience and perseverance required to become qualified to make history.

CHAPTER 7

Qualified for "Good Trouble"

After being elected to Congress, I was fortunate to spend time with Arthur Brooks, who was then the president of the American Enterprise Institute. His decade at the helm of AEI was a model of what leadership looked like. He was a great mentor in helping me decide how and where to raise my voice.

Arthur continually tried to convince conservatives and liberals to have a different kind of discussion. He would tell individuals and even entire organizations, "Go where you're not welcome. Get out of your comfort zone!

Expand your horizons, and engage with true believers, persuadables, and even hostiles."

To be clear, he wasn't saying go into places and pick a fight but was saying that preaching only to your own choir is no longer an option if you want to lead and make a difference. He suggested that leadership requires the willingness to go into unconventional places, the courage to share principles with those who disagree, and the confidence to stand up and speak out even in the face of overwhelming opposition.

Finding leaders who are willing to go to hard places is increasingly difficult. Far too many leaders prefer to stay in the safe and sanitized spaces where consultants and staff can control everything and prevent the leader from having an uncomfortable or potential gaffe-producing moment.

On the night of the assassination of Martin Luther King Jr., Bobby Kennedy, against the advice of his handlers and security team, went into an intercity ghetto to address an already angry, weary, and devastated crowd. Standing in the back of a pickup truck, in a hostile environment, Kennedy delivered from scribbled notes the news of Dr. King's tragic death. Then he powerfully issued an inspired call to unity. It is one of the most powerful speeches ever given because Kennedy was willing to go into a difficult spot.

Everyone should take a minute and read this very short, yet transcendent speech in its entirety:

Ladies and Gentlemen,

I'm only going to talk to you just for a minute or so this evening because I have some very sad news for all of you. Could you lower those signs, please? I have some very sad news for all of you and, I think, sad news for all of our fellow citizens and people who love peace all over the world, and that is that Martin Luther King was shot and was killed tonight in Memphis, Tennessee.

Martin Luther King dedicated his life to love and to justice between fellow human beings. He died in the cause of that effort. In this difficult day, in this difficult time for the United States, it's perhaps well to ask what kind of a nation we are and what direction we want to move in.

For those of you who are black—considering the evidence evidently is that there were white people who were responsible—you can be filled with bitterness, and with hatred, and a desire for revenge.

We can move in that direction as a country, in greater polarization—black people amongst blacks, and white amongst whites, filled with hatred toward one another. Or we can make an effort, as Martin Luther King did, to understand and to comprehend, and replace that violence, that stain of bloodshed that has spread across our land, with an effort to understand, compassion, and love.

For those of you who are black and are tempted to be filled with hatred and distrust at the injustice of such an act, against all white people, I would only say that I can also feel in my own heart the same kind of feeling. I had a member of my family killed, but he was killed by a white man.

But we have to make an effort in the United States. We have to make an effort to understand, to get beyond, to go beyond these rather difficult times.

My favorite poet was Aeschylus. And he once wrote:

"Even in our sleep, pain which cannot forget falls drop by drop upon the heart, until, in our own despair, against our will, comes wisdom through the awful grace of God."

What we need in the United States is not division; what we need in the United States is not hatred; what we need in the United States is not violence and lawlessness, but love, and wisdom, and compassion toward one another, and a feeling of justice toward those who still suffer within our country, whether they be white or whether they be black.

So I shall ask you tonight to return home,

to say a prayer for the family of Martin Luther King—yeah, it's true—but more importantly to say a prayer for our own country, which all of us love a prayer for understanding and that compassion of which I spoke.

We can do well in this country. We will have difficult times. We've had difficult times in the past; and we will have difficult times in the future. It is not the end of violence; it is not the end of lawlessness; and it's not the end of disorder.

But the vast majority of white people and the vast majority of black people in this country want to live together, want to improve the quality of our life, and want justice for all human beings that abide in our land.

And let's dedicate ourselves to what the Greeks wrote so many years ago: to tame the savageness of man and make gentle the life of this world. Let us dedicate ourselves to that, and say a prayer for our country and for our people.

Thank you very much.[1]

While moments such as Kennedy's speech are rare, the opportunities to go where you, or your principles and ideas, may not be welcomed are plenty.

As the only female Republican member of the Congressional Black Caucus, I had the opportunity every day to work across the aisle on issues that are divisive but important. My willingness to go into the CBC may have taken a little courage from me at the beginning, but I soon realized that I was the one being blessed. While I was willing to step into an unknown space, it was the kindness, grace, and vision of others that made it all work. The first few steps into the CBC were tenuous and uncertain for me. For the members of the CBC who didn't know me, there was some understandable suspicion and worry.

Representative Marcia Fudge, a Democrat from Ohio, was the outgoing chair of the CBC. I had come to know her through Representative Joyce Beatty, a Democrat from Ohio. Marcia was the first member who told the rest of the group, "Listen, I will look after Mia. We are going to invite her to come, and I want her to participate." That was an important lesson in trust. Marcia was willing to put her reputation on the line to create space for me.

Interestingly, my first encounter with the Congressional Black Caucus was with the women of the CBC as they were doing a photo shoot for *Essence* magazine. The shoot was a wonderful, nonpolitical, nonthreatening space to begin to build relationships. We talked and talked and talked, and then we took the picture.

In those conversations I recognized that the women of the CBC were interested in not only politics and policy.

What they wanted to know about me was whether or not I would take any of them to dinner. Not in the "who is going to pick up the check" kind of way—but something much deeper, more sisterly. The work of the CBC mattered to each of them, but they weren't interested in just interacting with you in meetings. These women wanted to know and learn from each other outside of the congressional halls. The phrase "Are you going to take them to dinner?" became an important questioning principle for me with the CBC and others throughout my time in Washington. When people know that you're going to take them to dinner, that you are genuinely interested in them beyond politics—everything changes.

I sat next to Marcia Fudge in our meetings because I felt comfortable. I felt safe with her, and her willingness to sit next to me, the newest and most unconventional member of the CBC, showed the kind of courage and grace we need more of in our nation's capital.

There were of course some growing pains as things progressed. Representative G. K. Butterfield, a Democrat from North Carolina, was the incoming chair. As the work of the CBC was discussed, there were some very tense moments in those early meetings.

Often it would play out like this: An issue would be raised, and someone would say, "Well, we're going to have to wait to discuss this." Or, "I don't think we should talk about this with present company." All eyes would look my way, followed by an intense and awkward silence that would seemingly last for hours. Finally, G. K. would say, "Well, I'm sorry, but we're just gonna have to...we're just gonna have to have you leave." That certainly didn't feel right to me, and it didn't feel right to many of the members.

While the "will you take me out to dinner" served to express the interest in having a relationship with individual members, it was another food moment that propelled my membership in the CBC forward.

Every Wednesday, the CBC serves a meal. It is a big deal to CBC members. It is a meal that each member brings in that tells the others a little bit about who you are and where you are from. I do remember that everyone joked about former representative Allen West, a Republican from Georgia, bringing in Chick-fil-A. I knew I was going to bring in Haitian food when it was my turn.

I remember eating pork chops once, and I think it might have been Representative Hank Johnson, a Democrat from Georgia, who brought it in. I was completely engaged in eating this wonderful food when the uncomfortable silence, stares, and "I think we should have you leave now" moment came. I had my own moment; I no longer wanted to feel that I was being tolerated in this group, that I didn't really belong and that they didn't want me there.

Filtering is not always my strong suit. So I said what I

was thinking out loud: "I don't want to be where I'm not wanted. But this is not going to bode well. I'm part of the Congressional Black Caucus. You can't just kick me out."

I had a meeting with Chairman Butterfield. I said, "Listen, I'm not here trying to blow you up, or have you do that to me. We're going to have to come up with something better than the current approach." I told him that if I were kicked out of the CBC, which is supposed to be nonpartisan, and if the media asked, I would have to tell them honestly that I got kicked out.

I went on to express that I didn't have any interest at all in being at odds with him as the chair or the CBC as a whole. We had to come up with some way for the meetings to be productive and for mutual trust to flourish.

Chairman Butterfield came up with a great path for us to pursue. He asked how I would feel if the CBC meetings were adjourned, and then they could go into a Democrat caucus meeting? I was just fine with that, since it would allow me to say truthfully that I had never been kicked out of a CBC meeting. It was a great compromise.

Shortly after that conversation with Chairman Butterfield, I remember getting on the floor that day feeling like things had been sufficiently settled. I really didn't want to be at odds with anyone in the CBC, and I also didn't want to feel like I wasn't fully part of CBC meetings.

I remember standing there when CBC member Hank Johnson came up to me. He said, "Mia Love, they didn't let you finish your pork chop! That makes me mad." He was really upset that they kicked me out, since he perceived that they had kicked me out of that meeting without even letting me finish my meal. He said he told his colleagues, "This is not right. You need to let this lady finish her meal before you decide that you're going to kick her out."

I didn't know Hank Johnson very well at that point—only that he was a fierce partisan. I admit I sort of braced for impact. But he came to me that day in kindness, compassion, and understanding. I told him we had figured it out and that we were all going to be okay.

While I often didn't finish my meals at our CBC meetings, it wasn't because I didn't have the chance. Compassion, compromise, and kindness led to a level of trust that surprised us all.

Here's the really interesting part. As time went on, the chair stopped adjourning the Congressional Black Caucus meeting, even when talking about more partisan issues. Members said whatever they wanted to, because they knew and trusted that I would keep whatever happened in the meeting in the meeting. It was clear that if we had any battles as a CBC family, we were going to have it in the room, not outside. I never, ever heard them talk ill of me outside of that meeting, and I did the same for them. Outside of that meeting, it was more of a brotherhood and sisterhood for which I will forever be thankful.

Leading up to the State of the Union Address in 2018, Representative Cedric Richmond, a Democrat from Louisiana, and I had a number of what I believed were crucial conversations. Cedric, at that time, was running to be the next chair of the CBC and wanted my support. I really liked Representative Richmond, and we had many important conversations. I told him that I believed the Congressional Black Caucus could be an even more powerful group if it could stand on its own and if it were not seen as a group used as a tool by the left. For instance, I pointed out that there was an appropriations bill battle going on in Congress. The Democratic Caucus wanted to stop the appropriations bill, so they had the CBC bring a Confederate flag issue into the debate that really had nothing to do with the CBC; it had everything to do with stopping the appropriations bill. The CBC knew that. I told Cedric that he had to get to the point where the CBC was willing to give votes to Republicans, if it meant that it helped the Black community.

We discussed that there were really so very many opportunities to transcend the typical Democrat versus Republican battles. When we do that, then people would know what the CBC was really all about, and then people would come to the CBC instead of bypassing or engaging only when it met partisan needs.

Following the State of the Union Address, my husband Jason and I were visiting with Representative Richmond.

The conversation ultimately led us to talking about our party differences and why we affiliated with our particular party. This led to an amazing "wow" moment for me.

Representative Richmond said, "Mia, why you are a Republican is truly interesting to me. You believe in a lot of the things we Democrats believe in. So, explain it to me."

I reminded him that my parents are from Haiti. I recounted how they grew up and how the government suppressed and stopped them from thriving through one corrupt dictatorship after another. For my parents in Haiti, it was all about government. It was impossible for an individual to start a business. And I told him that my parents didn't want a big and corrupt government to dictate their lives, fortune, or future. When they had the opportunity to come to the United States, they just wanted the opportunity to work and feed their families without having a government stop them from pursuing or achieving their dreams.

I also shared how being on a city council and then serving as a mayor demonstrated to me that the best solutions are found at the most local level—that you can take care of people easier and more efficiently and more effectively at a local level. I concluded by restating that I am always for bigger people and less government—the way the Constitution was set up with a government for, of, and by the people.

At this point, Jason jumped in and asked Representative Richmond, "Can you tell us why you are a Democrat?" His response opened my eyes in a new way. He began, "It is funny how all of your experiences led you to push for bigger people, less government, more local control. My experience growing up in Alabama was very, very different."

Cedric continued, saying, "It was the local authorities in Alabama that wouldn't allow Black people to vote. It was the local police officers that were beating our families, our uncles, our aunts, our mothers, and our fathers with clubs, throwing them in jail and whipping them on the streets. Doing all this as they attempted to march peacefully for progress, dignity, and equality. The people I cared about were beaten up by the local government, and it was actually the federal government that stepped in to protect them. It was the federal government that enforced the idea that all were created equal."

He concluded, "I don't have as much faith in local governments as you have." I had never seen it from that perspective, but I instantly came to understand the source of his distrust. Having a great understanding of where each of us came from and what shaped our thinking was absolutely transformational.

Representative Richmond and I would have these conversations on and off over time. They were a great blessing to me and even helped improve the way the CBC worked. As a matter of fact, there were times when my CBC colleagues would ask me what I thought the Republican conference was going to do on a particular issue or where they were trying to go. Without betraying any confidence or loyalty to my own party, I became a source of information, ideas, and questions that would be helpful in working toward better policy, greater compromise, and better understanding. I had a familial love for the members of the CBC. I will never forget the kindness and prayers we shared with and for one another. They looked out for me, and I did the same for them. There are some bonds that politics cannot break.

———————————

The title of this chapter is a tribute to someone I likely wouldn't have connected with had I not chosen to step into that unique place. The late John Lewis, who represented Georgia as a Democrat, is an icon in America's march toward justice and equality. Pages and volumes have been dedicated to his life, sacrifice, and service to our country. John Lewis owned his story, found his voice, raised it, led with character, and helped countless others to do the same.

John was famous for "good trouble." It was really his way of demonstrating that you have to be willing to do things differently if you want to leave your mark on the world and make it better in the process.

I could fill an entire book with what I learned from John Lewis.

John Lewis always greeted me the same when we would run into each other or attend meetings. He would say, "How are you doing? How are your babies? Are your babies doing good? Are you doing good?" He genuinely wanted to know. His questions helped me feel like I belonged.

I remember flying home to Utah once, and Representative Lewis was on the first leg with me from Washington to Atlanta. John was sitting in first class, and I was sitting directly behind him in comfort class. During the flight he engaged in a conversation, and per usual he asked how my babies were doing and how I was doing.

John asked if I was heading home. I said that I was hoping to make it home, but since our flight was delayed getting out of Washington, I might miss my connection in Atlanta. He was so positive and assured me I was going to make my next flight and that I would get home to my family in Utah.

As the flight went on, I was amazed at how gracious the congressman was. So many came up to thank him for his service, for his example, for his strength. John always made time for everyone, especially for the children. I am sure he was tired, and I am sure he would have enjoyed a

few minutes of peace and quiet. He made time for everyone and made sure that everyone felt special. That was a
lesson for me.

We finally landed in Atlanta. I was beyond doubtful
that I would be able to make my connecting flight. Of
course, almost everyone landing in Atlanta on the plane
had a connection to run for. If ever the phrase "Every
man or woman for themselves" applies, it is while deplan-
ing in Atlanta when flights have been delayed.

John Lewis was not a large man, and he had a very
quiet voice. As the rest of the passengers started to grab
their bags out of the overhead bins and jostle for position for a quick exit, John Lewis softly said, "Ladies and
gentlemen." Everyone, and I mean everyone, froze. He
continued, "This young lady is trying to get home to her
children tonight. Would you please let her by so she can
make her connection and be able to get to her kids?"

Immediately, the aisle of the plane parted like the
Red Sea. John said, "Go ahead, my friend, get home to
your kids." He gave me a kiss on the cheek and sent me
on my way.

John didn't care if any reporters or politicos saw his
act of kindness to a Republican from Utah. He always
did the right thing because it was the right thing—period.

I did make my flight. I did make it home to my babies.
I did remember the "good trouble" John had caused for
me—because it was the right thing for him to do.

John Lewis and I came from very different backgrounds, political perspectives, and life experiences. But
he showed me that kindness is king. He taught me that
if you haven't walked in someone else's shoes, you really
don't know what you don't know.

One of my other "good trouble" friends was Representative Emanuel Cleaver, a Democrat from Missouri.
We often just called him Rev. because he was also an
ordained minister, and he could preach with the best
of them.

Representative Cleaver and I connected on a number
of issues, including the need to better assist those facing poverty. Democrats have long been seen as the party
that is most helpful to the poor. I often questioned that
because I had seen so many who had become trapped
in government programs that seemed to provide them
exactly what they needed to stay right where they
were. There was no path up or out of poverty. In fact,
in many instances there were significant penalties for
progress.

Rev. and I both believed that the key to eradicating
poverty was to make sure that we didn't treat those in
poverty as liabilities to be managed but as human assets
with unlimited potential to be developed.

One of the benefits of living in Utah is that there
are many examples of upward mobility and how to lift
those who are struggling, strengthen them with skills,

and empower them to take advantage of opportunities that rise.

I invited the congressman to come join me in Utah for a summit on poverty. He agreed, and things were lining up. Just prior to his trip there was a major showdown in Washington over guns. I believe he was pressured to cancel the trip because we had different views about the Second Amendment. But Rev. kept his commitment, and we had a wonderful experience.

Some members of the meeting wanted to focus on our differences, whether Representative Cleaver would support a Republican like me. In his classic grace, he said we are not obsessing on the areas where we disagree. We are focusing on opportunities to make a difference for those facing poverty.

In our summit we talked about the need to approach generational poverty differently from situational poverty. Too often they were being treated the same, which was producing bad outcomes.

Together, we toured Welfare Square of The Church of Jesus Christ of Latter-day Saints and met with business and community leaders. I was pleased to have Rep. Cleaver actually experience for himself what the Church describes this way:

Welfare Square is a landmark location for The Church of Jesus Christ of Latter-day Saints in its efforts to care for those in need. The square hosts various employment services, food production and storage facilities, distribution centers, and training facilities. The services housed here are provided free of charge to Latter-day Saints and others in the community...

Welfare Square resides on its own campus and includes a 178-foot grain silo, a milk and cheese processing plant, a cannery, a bakery, a market-style grocery, a clothing collection warehouse, and employment assistance offices. Services on the square are operated by volunteers and employees of the Church.[2]

Representative Cleaver, who grew up in real poverty, came to understand and appreciate the approach of self-reliance, life skills, and community-driven solutions.

Had we focused solely on the areas where we disagreed, we both would have missed out on priceless principles and shared policy approaches that made a difference and led to many other wonderful conversations and collaborations.

Being willing to get into some "good trouble" was important throughout my time in Congress. My main goal was to see real change take place and be intentional and purposeful with the time I had in office. That vision enabled me to work with anyone and everyone on particular pieces of legislation without worrying about what the party bosses or the media would say.

In April 2016, I saw my first bill pass, which raised limits on how large community banks can grow. I believed this would make more credit available. This was important to me because I recognized how hard it could be for some people to get access to credit from big banks. I had also seen the devastation of predatory lending that took advantage of young mothers trying to buy formula for a baby but having to get a payday loan at ridiculous interest rates just to make it to their next paycheck.

I was a lead sponsor for the Student Right to Know Before You Go Act to help prospective college students understand how much their degree was going to cost them and what their chances were of earning enough post-graduation to pay off their loans. I also cosponsored the Affordable College Textbook Act.

In December 2017, I introduced the Stop Taxpayers Obligations to Perpetrators of Sexual Harassment Act, which passed in February 2018 and prevented members of Congress from settling sexual harassment claims with taxpayer money.

I was a supporter of creating laws against pyramid schemes and adding multivitamins to the list of items food stamps would buy. I also advocated on several fronts for desperately needed immigration reform.

So many of these laws required alliances and conversations across the aisle.

During my time as a member of the House of Representatives, my duty was to represent the people who needed a voice. My platform was a list of beliefs that I personally believed in. I believed it was my duty to fight to protect life at all stages, preserve free markets, promote fiscal responsibility, and limit government power.

Above all, I was dedicated to using my voice, attempting to lead with character, and promoting good policies that would empower citizens—especially those who had no voice—to rise to the measure of their potential. Sometimes that required me to go against my party or the prevailing political winds. Often it wasn't popular.

Following such a path landed me in some political trouble—"good trouble"! Thanks, John.

CHAPTER 8

"So You're Telling Me There's a Chance"

In the 1994 cult movie *Dumb and Dumber*, Lloyd Christmas (Jim Carrey) works as a limo driver and falls in love with a woman named Mary Swanson (Lauren Holly), whom he is driving to the airport. Lloyd and Mary are worlds apart in almost every way, and a star-crossed comedy of errors ensues.

At one point, Lloyd confesses his love for Mary and asks if she shares his belief that they have a future together. Mary tells him the odds are one in a million. To which Lloyd enthusiastically replies, "So you're telling me there's a chance!"

There is a positive message in Lloyd's belief in one in a million.

As I expressed in earlier chapters, the great breakthroughs and triumphs of America have often come in the most unlikely moments. Moments of high risk, uncertainty, and long odds seem to be fertile ground for harvesting heroines and heroes in America.

Courage is displayed and character is revealed not when victory is certain, but when the odds of success are beyond one in a million. But in America's rich history, in each unlikely, improbably, impossible instance, someone believed they were qualified—usually by the content of their character—and enthusiastically responded, "So you're telling me there's a chance!"

I love that about America. There is always a chance. Although I and my family are proud to call ourselves American citizens and are proud to live in a country full of such promise, I am not blind to the failings and long-time barriers within the system. Sometimes our flaws as a nation seem to outweigh all the lives lifted, opportunities promised, and success realized in the history of our constitutional republic.

There is still change that needs to happen and areas that need to be fixed. We have to be willing to step into that space without condemning the entirety of the American experiment and system just because we have not always lived up to those principles professed by the founders and enshrined in our founding documents.

I became willing and determined to put the work in to see the results I wanted to see in my own life and for my own family.

Many moments of my life had discouraging and depressing odds of more than one in a million. And yet, there was always a chance.

I am but one of millions, actually, who have beat the odds *because* in America there is always a chance.

The great baseball player and color-barrier breaker Jackie Robinson entered Major League Baseball in 1947. His odds were well beyond one in a million to make it to the big leagues. Robinson endured taunts, slurs, and abuses of every kind. And yet he kept his belief, not only in his personal professional goals, but in a vision of the kind of equality that could unite the nation.

Several years later, Robinson participated in a radio essay program called *This I Believe*. He described his fight and what gave him hope, saying:

> Whatever obstacles I found made me fight all the harder. But it would have been impossible for me to fight at all, except that I was sustained by the personal and deep-rooted belief that my fight had a chance. *It had a chance because it took place in a free society. Not once was I forced to face and*

fight an immovable object. Not once was the situation so cast-iron rigid that I had no chance at all.

Robinson concluded with what he believed would be the reality for his children and their children:

I can say to my children: There is a chance for you. No guarantee, but a chance...

But I do believe—and with every fiber in me—that what I was able to attain came to be because we put behind us (no matter how slowly) the dogmas of the past: to discover the truth of today; and perhaps find the greatness of tomorrow.[1] [Emphasis added.]

———————

Because of my parents' dream for a better life in America, I know that change and a better future is possible with hard work and determination. As I recognized that I grew up in what many would call a ghetto of America, I became determined to strive for a better life of my own. I did not allow my humble background to deter me from my chances of success, but rather allowed it to inspire me to greater success. I chose to believe in the promise of the American Dream, instead of believing it is an empty promise.

I spoke to so many Americans who were tired of having the government give them exactly what they needed to stay exactly where they were. Like my dad, most Americans just want you to tell them, with honesty and certainty, that they have a chance.

President Abraham Lincoln declared that the role of government was "to elevate the condition of men; to lift artificial weights from all shoulders; to clear the paths of laudable pursuit for all; to afford all an unfettered start and a fair chance in the race of life."[2]

I really started to think about the chances Lincoln described when I traveled with Representative Elijah Cummings, a Democrat from Maryland, to Baltimore. We visited a portion of the district he represented.

The visits to other members' districts were always enjoyable and instructive for me. This visit started in typical fashion with a stop at a business—it just happened to be Amazon. Representative Cummings was supportive of Amazon and its workers, and there was a great question-and-answer session where I again gained insight from hardworking people and from a representative who clearly cared for those who had sent him to Congress.

Later in the day, we had the opportunity to go into the projects—Section Eight housing. I admit that even with my background, walking through it was really surreal. Representative Cummings felt very comfortable just walking through and talking to people, sincerely asking, "How are you doing? How's it going?"

Representative Cummings was known for being very tough, and his tough exterior just added to his larger-than-life persona. When you really got to know him, you came to understand that he was really kind. He was a friend to all. He also had one of those political odd-couple relationships in his loyal friendship with Mark Meadows, a Republican from North Carolina. They were two people from very opposite ends of the aisle who really had a genuine friendship. I admired that. Watching him interact with a variety of people gave me a high level of trust in him.

As we walked along and observed the conditions and the people, the thought kept coming to my mind that this was supposed to be just a temporary, not a permanent, place for those in need. It was designed to be a place that would be safe and enable individuals and families to get out and move up in their lives.

These thoughts prompted me to pull a woman aside. I asked if she would be willing to talk to me for a little bit about what life was like in this place. She said she was willing and pulled me into her kitchen and had me sit down. Representative Cummings and the others in our group went off somewhere else while I listened to this woman.

I repeated my question: "Tell me about what typical

life is like." She replied, saying, "Let me tell you what typical life is like for my little girl." She continued, "You see that pink coat over there? I bought her that pink coat. Because I wanted her to feel good about something. I couldn't afford it. I couldn't afford that pink coat. But when my little girl saw it, she liked it."

Her voice dropped as she explained, "I wanted her to wrap herself in something that made her feel good. Because you only know what you know. Let me tell you what my little girl knows. She puts on her coat every day. And she walks out into the hall, and she has to hop over people that may be lying, especially on a Monday, that may be lying in the hall, because they're passed out from a night of heavy drinking. She walks into a urine-filled elevator to get outside. Then she has to avoid every thug, every bad person that is just wanting to mess with her, beat her up, hassle her, and heaven knows what else they want to do. She has to get through that."

I found my heart racing and aching. I wanted her to be done, but she wasn't as she said, "Then, once she gets to school, finally, she has to go through metal detectors. And when she eventually gets to her classroom, she sits down with a teacher who is too tired and too overworked to really put in the time and the effort that she and her classmates need to inspire them to learn. After school my little girl, and many just like her, go through all of those things again as they try to get safely home. Same people in the hall, same urine-filled elevators, same thugs. I bought her that coat in the hopes that she can remember the stories I'm telling her at home as she moves through the world she knows."

I asked what kind of stories the woman told her little girl. She replied, "I tell her dreams about living outside. What a nice house looks like. What a playground looks like. What a world with no elevators, no people lying on the streets or lying in the halls looks like. I describe places where you can walk out on some grass, get on the bus, go to school, go to a nice school where you're not met with metal detectors, and sit down with a teacher that is excited and inspired to teach you."

The mother's voice was rising, and my heart was racing while considering that this life could be a reality. She continued her story: "I tell her stories of learning amazing things at school. That she can learn how to make things, how to solve problems. I tell her about all of those kinds of things."

This heroic mom said, "And I tell her those things in the hope that she doesn't just remember what she's going through day to day, because you only know what you see, you only know what you experience."

She realized she had my full attention, and my heart. She continued, saying, "Now you know what life is like here. You want to know how to make things better?

This doesn't make things better." She asked, "Why is it that people only give you just so much to go so far? Why is it that every time I want to make a little bit more money I face the risk of losing the roof over my head? Is it so I can't do any more or rise up? Why is it that I can't save enough money so I can buy my own car? Why is it that I can't save money so maybe I can give my little girl that house? Why can't I get out of here so I can get her to that different school with a teacher that's not too tired?"

This was a master class for the ages. I was being taught by a most extraordinary woman. And that was when it dawned on me. That's when I thought to myself, Government gives you exactly what you need to stay exactly where you are. To go no further. Too many poverty programs keep people trapped. The world that they know is the only thing that they see. No one can aspire to more because they haven't seen anything more.

That mom, thank goodness for her, tells her daughter a different story and wraps her in a pink coat to keep it all in tight in the hopes that she can make those stories her reality and find a way out.

Maybe that little girl becomes a teacher who can inspire others. Maybe she learns how to solve the problem. Maybe that little girl breaks out of a system that failed her family. Maybe she gets a scholarship, goes somewhere, and comes full circle by getting her mom out

High school graduation, with my father and mother, Jean Maxine and Marie Bourdeau.

With my father on the evening of my high school prom. I'm wearing the red dress that Marc and Donna McKenzie bought for me.

Performing with the Norwalk High School Color Guard.

At the Norwalk High School Marching Band awards ceremony with my instructor, Jeffery Smith.

Left: With my dad and daughter Abi at my mayoral inauguration event in Saratoga Springs, Utah.

Below: Giving my speech at the 2012 Republican National Convention in Tampa, Florida. "That's the America I know—because we built it!" I knew I was prepared to deliver a great speech, but I had no idea what my words would mean to people across the country. *(Reuters)*

Right after winning the race for Utah's 4th congressional district in 2014. My parents were so proud of my history-making win as the first Black Republican woman ever elected to Congress. *(Jeremy Harmon and the Salt Lake Tribune)*

Me, Jason, and our children during the campaign years. Running and serving in Congress was a family effort, and they have always been my biggest support system.

Being sworn in with my mom, Speaker of the House Paul Ryan, Jason, and Jean Claude Jean (my second dad).

Paul Ryan pinning the congressional pin on my lapel. The Speaker was my assigned mentor, and he became a trusted advisor and big brother to me.

Jason and me in front of my new congressional office in the Rayburn House Office Building. This was a surreal moment for both of us.

I was so honored to present Congressman Elijah Cummings with his family history, which had been assembled by The Church of Jesus Christ of Latter-day Saints.

Among a sea of white men during congressional committee hearings.

My husband, Jason, is
the best human being
I know and the most
amazing life partner.

Serving in Congress is not a glamorous job. I spent long hours in my DC office because I needed to make the time away from my family count.

With Jason Chaffetz, Mark Walker, Trey Gowdy, and John Ratcliffe. I am so thankful for the group of friends that I made while in Congress, whose feedback and advice were invaluable to me.

Left: Senator Tim Scott became a trusted colleague and friend. We snapped this selfie when I was visiting his office in DC recently. I'm so thankful that there are still good people like Tim Scott in Washington.

Below: With Joshua Holt, one of my constituents, who had been wrongfully imprisoned in Venezuela for over a year. Josh and his family became dear friends and were some of my biggest supporters during my 2018 campaign.

Left: Laurie Holt, Joshua's mother and my dear friend. Laurie passed away in 2019. I miss her.

Below: With Haitian President Jovenel Moïse and my father when I visited Haiti in 2017. I was devastated to learn of the assassination of President Moïse in 2021.

My visit to Juab High School. I thoroughly enjoyed the opportunity to speak with high school students all over my district.

With one of our amazing veterans from Utah's 4th congressional district. Veterans' issues were a top priority for me.

Left: One of my many visits to businesses in my district.

Below: I had so many opportunities to interact with veterans from my district. I have enormous respect and love for anyone who has served our country.

Above: The Poverty Summit, which Congressman Emanuel Cleaver and I hosted in Salt Lake City, Utah.

Left: My family enjoys the outdoor lifestyle and the beauty of Utah's landscapes. This photo was taken in Moab, Utah.

Jason and me at
Arches National Park.

With my son,
Peyton, and our
matching dunks.

Left: At a press conference after my congressional loss in 2018, with Jason and my parents.

Below: At a Young America's Foundation event in Washington, DC. I take every opportunity to speak to young Americans and remind them of their potential and the importance for them to be politically involved.

On the streets of New York City prior to an appearance on *The View*.

of that place. We need to make sure that every little girl in a pink coat can be lifted, empowered, and strengthened to be as extraordinary as she chooses to be.

It's not enough to give people exactly what they need to stay exactly where they are. We have to provide both the vision and the resources so that they can rightly say about their big dreams, "So you're saying there's a chance!"

I have tried to follow Lincoln's motto for the proper role of government throughout my time in public office. If I could clear a path or provide an unfettered start, I was helping to declare that there was truly a chance, a fair chance to win this race of life—for everyone.

———————

I am no Jackie Robinson, but I learned some extraordinary lessons about how there actually was a way to build bridges and get to bipartisan relationships—through softball! Congressional softball.

The first day I stepped on the floor of the House of Representatives, the only thing that the Democrats wanted to talk to me about was the Congress-versus-the-press softball game. I admit it wasn't on my radar and wasn't something I really wanted to do.

I remember Kyrsten Sinema, then a Democratic House member from Arizona, telling me that I really should play because it was for a good cause. She said it was one of the only things that members do together that is actually worth something. (I felt really sad about that!) Sinema and I really connected, and we worked on a whole lot of issues together as a result.

I finally relented, and when I went to the practice, they realized I could run pretty fast. I was in. It was through softball that I got to know Representative Debbie Wasserman Schultz, a Democrat from Florida. Debbie and I discussed a wide array of things, including her breast cancer diagnosis. We talked about the women whom we were going to help. When you actually have conversations about real life in a real-life setting, not a political setting, relationships start to change.

In the middle of that first season, Representative Wasserman Schultz came up to me and said, "On paper, political paper, I thought I was going to hate you. I thought you and I would never get along. I cannot believe that we get along this well."

Not surprisingly, when you just start looking for things that you actually have in common and issues you want to work together on—everything changes. I remember that Debbie saw me on CNN once and she told me, "I don't agree with everything you said. But I really appreciate the tone."

I never would have guessed that softball could be such a uniting force in Congress. We need a lot more softball in Washington and in our communities; the shift from looking for the negative in those we may disagree with can happen in any aspect in life.

I mean, Representative Cheri Bustos, a Democrat from Illinois, and I connected on a number of issues because of our relationship in softball. More important than politics, I remember walking into the hallway of the House Cannon building once to see Representative Bustos throwing a football across the hall with my son Peyton. Every time Peyton came to Washington, he would ask where his football friend was.

I also had my Republican friends there too: Martha Roby from Alabama and Martha McSally from Arizona, as well as others. When you get women who are playing softball together and doing things that bring in other women and help those who have suffered from cancer, the cause becomes bigger than yourself. That's what Washington needs.

Representative Cummings taught me plenty about the power of connecting people to other people and how that connected them to opportunities. I was thankful that I was given the chance to help Representative Cummings connect to his own one-in-a-million-chance story and history. The Church of Jesus Christ of Latter-day Saints has one of the most extensive family history and genealogical resources in the world. Church leaders allowed me to pick two people in the Congressional Black Caucus to have a significant genealogical family history assembled. The Church will do this on occasion for special visitors, guests, and dignitaries. It represents immense work and shows the power of connecting across the generations. I chose Marcia Fudge and Elijah Cummings.

Genealogy, family history, and personal story are incredibly important to members of the Congressional Black Caucus. Connecting to ancestry is vital.

Not long after I had presented Representative Cummings with his family history, he came and found me on the House floor; he was very excited. He said, "Mia, I can't believe how much this history has helped me." It had personal letters that he was able to copy and print and share with his family, which he was thrilled about.

More important, he found that a lot of men in his family didn't live past the age of fifty because they had heart trouble. Elijah had heart trouble as well. He showed his history to his doctor with some of the detailed information. The doctor said, "Oh, my gosh, I think we might now know what's wrong with you." Representative Cummings had a heart condition that he inherited. And he would not have known that specific condition otherwise.

A very thankful Representative Cummings said, "Mia, you might have just saved my life, you and your church might have saved my life." Fortunately, he stayed with us for several more, very important years, during which his influence and impact were tremendous.

Marcia Fudge's history went back past six generations. Some of her ancestors were married, but their marriages weren't documented because they were illegal. And she was actually able to see on the pages of this history what connected so many amazing dots, lives, and people together.

After that, of course, every single CBC member wanted a history. I opened some of their eyes to the fact that The Church of Jesus Christ of Latter-day Saints actually partnered with the National Museum of African American History and Culture, and that the whole second floor, through collaboration with the Church's FamilySearch.org website, can actually do the family history and genealogy work there. It is a place where countless one-in-a-million histories are written. We should recognize that because we live in America, we always have a chance. Senator Tim Scott, a Republican from South Carolina, has called his story "From Cotton to Congress,"[3] and Supreme Court Justice Ketanji Brown Jackson called her journey "From Segregation to the Supreme Court."[4]

Qualified

Regardless of who you are, where you are from, or what your background, race, religion, or creed might include—you can rise, you can overcome, and you can achieve.

Despite your flaws, failures, and a host of problems to overcome, I am telling you that because you live in America—there's a chance!

CHAPTER 9

Declaring Your Character in an Age of Reputation

Throughout my life, from growing up in Connecticut to walking through the halls of Congress, I have learned about and tried to focus on developing my character. I love the quote from John Wooden: "Be more concerned with your character than your reputation. Character is what you really are; reputation is what you are perceived to be."[1]

In this chapter, I want to share some of the things I

learned about character, happiness, and successful living during my time in Congress.

In a world with a 24/7 news cycle, numerous people, politicians, celebrities, and business leaders spend an extraordinary amount of time managing their reputations. And while brand and reputation management are important disciplines, far too many are too concerned about them merely from a superficial standpoint. They are concerned with what everybody else thinks of them.

What everyone has to recognize is that your character or the character of your company is what matters most in the end. Your character will ultimately confirm that your reputation, good or bad, was right.

When you put your character first, everything else falls into place. Many individuals and companies have lost their way by changing their behavior or performance based on what their prevailing reputation was at the moment. This strategy usually leads to short-sighted decision-making, compromises in critical principles, and a never-ending attempt to please others.

It was during my campaign for the mayoral position in Saratoga Springs that I experienced the first political assault on my character. I also discovered that when you are explaining, you are losing. I also recognized, just like with my kids' sports teams, that if you are complaining about the rules or the referees, you are losing.

When the dust had settled from the mayoral primary

and we got into the general election for mayor, things got ugly. Mr. Jeff Francom alleged that my campaign sent political materials to his office that caused him to get fired from his job. I found myself facing a barrage of questions about Francom's preposterous claims on what seemed like a daily and even an hourly basis. I wanted to cry foul. I wanted to explain how ridiculous the allegation was. I wanted to go through point by point and refute his allegations. I wanted to share how unfair it was for me to have to answer these questions from reporters, in forums, town halls, and community events.

My trusty friend Deidre Henderson, who led Republican Jason Chaffetz's successful U.S. congressional campaign in Utah and now serves as the lieutenant governor of Utah, provided me with priceless counsel. She basically told me to stop explaining and step forward with confidence.

We came up with a short answer to the dishonest and harsh claims that was direct and closed the door to further questions on the matter. And that was that.

Most voters are smart enough to see past the smoke, desperate swings, and last-ditch manufactured scandals. I learned to trust voters. I had been going about it all wrong. I was trying to explain and ask the voters to trust me. In truth, what I needed to do was be direct and tell the voters that I trusted them to see the truth.

After the election, Francom's bosses released a

statement that he was fired for no other reason except he was bad at his job, and there had been no communication from my office at all. Sometimes validation comes late, but it usually comes. Truth does prevail. But waiting for it to prevail can be painful.

Unfortunately, that political attack on the content of my character was not my last. Throughout my time in Congress, I witnessed many dishonest individuals attempting to rig the system for their own personal gain.

Later in my career, after the White House Correspondents' Dinner and while I was in Texas working to raise money for my reelection to Congress, I received a call from my communications director. I was informed that I was being investigated by the media. They wanted to know if I had used taxpayer dollars to attend the event.

I knew for a fact that my campaign team and I had checked over and over again to explore all the specifics and details of the House Ethics Committee's policies and procedures. Right before the event, we checked one more time to make sure I was doing everything by the book. But when the story broke, it didn't matter. There was now a story.

This is one of the great tragedies of Washington, DC. Lies and innuendo are rapidly reported, but when they are proven false they are rarely, if ever, corrected. And even if a correction does come, it is often a year or more too late, and the damage is already done.

Your opponent can make up a story and get an ambitious or unscrupulous media member to publish it, true or false, right or wrong, and the story will become the narrative. If they can't find wrongdoing, some are more than willing to make it up.

I have always said and believed that a true friend always tells you the truth and helps you through turbulent times. Trey Gowdy, a Republican from South Carolina, was just such a friend for me in Congress.

I still have the pit in my stomach from the day I learned that papers were delivered to my office, from guys who looked like they were out of the *Men in Black* movies. I was informed that I was being investigated for an ethics violation that someone had submitted against me.

Such investigations were expensive and time-consuming, and often the allegations are filed anonymously for political purposes. I saw in the local paper that somebody complained about a correspondents' dinner I had attended. Whoever submitted the complaint clearly wanted me to get in trouble and have me pay a political price, regardless of whether or not any standards had been violated.

I remember talking to Trey about this. Trey said, "Mia, let me ask you something, point-blank. And you need to be honest with me. Did you do something wrong?"

And I told him I had done absolutely nothing wrong.

He thought for a moment and said, "Here is what

you're going to do. You're going to self-refer to the Ethics Committee. Take every possible charge or allegation, write it down, and go ask the Ethics Committee for guidance." And that was exactly what I did.

Interestingly, the Ethics Committee is the only committee in which Republicans and Democrats work together because members from both parties are equally vulnerable to the same political game.

Trey's advice and counsel were priceless. Getting in front of it wasn't just about getting in front of it. Asking for guidance, being humble enough to say, "Here are the things that I'm concerned about," and asking if I had done something wrong and if there was any corrective action required were the right things to do.

Ultimately, the Ethics Committee came back, saying that there was nothing wrong. Nothing needed to be corrected. I think it took about six months. Just as I can remember that pit in my stomach at the beginning, I remember the exhale and relief when I was informed that the case was closed!

That would have never happened without Trey's friendship and guidance. If I didn't have a good, trusted friend who had said, "Did you do anything wrong? Because if you did, we can fix it. But you have to be honest," things wouldn't have turned out well. He saved me from a lot of pain.

Sadly, this kind of anonymous complaint can cause

real political damage, cost hundreds of thousands of dollars, and take years to clear. In our rapid-fire world, the complaints—even when completely false or unfounded—leave a mark, while the absolute declaration of innocence can take years to confirm and rarely gets reported.

These games and attacks were the cause of much of my anxiety during my time as an elected official. I still remember the anxiety of receiving that call. There were others that were equally unfounded, and some literally took years before a statement was issued that my campaign and I had done things the right way and with complete transparency and integrity.

This is part of the problem in our politics—particularly with the "win at any cost" mindset of political power brokers in both parties. I learned in the end that you can't back down. You can't let the worries and threats from those who are interested in power more than they are interested in the truth scare you away from using your voice. You have to push through to make a difference.

A friend often reminded me, "You can't let the terrorists win!" Meaning, you can't let the bad guys and bullies shut you down.

Yes, there is truly corruption within the political realm. It was the most discouraging part of public life for me. I had such a hard time believing what some people were willing to do to win an election or cripple an opponent on an issue. I also saw candidates on both sides of the political aisle who truly cared about the principles, the policies, and the people they represented. Sadly, the corruption of the power brokers is driving many great women and men out of public service because the cost inflicted by relentless attacks on the content of their character was simply too high.

I regularly reminded voters, constituents, and my staff that it is the duty of each one of us to assess claims of misconduct and find out the truth for ourselves. In particular, I always warned supporters that toward the end of a campaign there was a "silly season" of desperation during which my character would be assaulted. I warned my loyal supporters to be prepared for the attacks that would come. I knew that personal, false, and distorted attacks would be thrown to distract and scare voters in order to slow our momentum and hurt our cause.

"Silly season" is just another name for the sad state of those willing to engage in the politics of personal destruction. Citizens should know better, and frankly they deserve better from those running for office.

I would half-jokingly tell voters that in the closing days of this campaign they would hear my opponent and big-money Washington allies say that I was going to push their grandmas off a cliff, that I didn't care about students, and they might even claim that I was going to outlaw ice cream and puppies. I would encourage voters to look closely at outrageous claims and remember that desperate is what desperate does.

I also took those moments to remind voters and supporters what character looks like and how my campaign was always about our positive message and the principles that make our nation extraordinary. I nearly begged campaign supporters to stay positive when attacks would come. Regardless of the negative nonsense the opposing campaign could conjure up and throw at me, I told them, check the real facts—and if what you heard from them didn't ring true, it was because it wasn't true.

My campaign simply had to maintain the high ground. We didn't need heated arguments and negativity of any kind. We needed to stick to our principles and the positive message that had put us in a position to lead and win to begin with.

Not letting the terrorists win with their lies and deceit is easy to say and hard to do, especially in the middle of a tightly contested race. But it still has to be done. I applaud all who chose to take that road less traveled. It is the road best traveled.

One additional bit of learning about true character in public service is understanding that the surest and swiftest way to fail and to lose your character is to try and please everybody all the time! You simply cannot be obsessed or concerned with what others think about you. We have an entire generation of politicians who are more worried about their online reputations, the number of likes and retweets they get, than they are about their integrity and character.

I loved what Senator Joe Manchin, a Democrat from West Virginia, said in the midst of relentless attacks—by members of his own political party—to get him to vote for legislation he simply did not support. Senator Manchin told his party leaders and the public for months that he could not support President Joe Biden's Build Back Better bill. Many were shocked that he didn't yield to the personal attacks and give in.

Senator Manchin often reminds people that being a senator is not the greatest job he has ever had and staying in office or the good graces of party bosses clearly isn't worth compromising his character. On one occasion he told *Forbes*' Andrew Solender: "This job's not worth it to me to sell my soul. What are you gonna do, vote me out? That's not a bad option, I get to go home."[2]

Even as far back as 1902, William George Jordan astutely pointed out, "The politician who is vacillating, temporizing, shifting, constantly trimming his sails to catch every puff of wind of popularity, is a trickster who succeeds only until he is found out. A lie may live for a time, truth for all time. A lie never lives by its own vitality, it merely continues to exist because it simulates truth. When it is unmasked, it dies."

In a warning for leaders of every era, Jordan concluded, "Men who split hairs with their conscience, who mislead others by deft, shrewd phrasing...designedly uttered to produce a false impression, are untruthful in the most cowardly way...They forgive themselves their crime in congratulating themselves on the cleverness of their alibi."[3]

Watching the continued lack of courage and leadership in Washington today, I am reminded of the well-known scene in the movie *A Man for All Seasons* where Sir Thomas More delivers one of the most powerful and poignant lines of all time. More had been betrayed by Richard Rich, who, after falsely testifying against More, was rewarded by being made the equivalent of the attorney general for Wales. More confronts his betrayer with: "Why Richard, it profits a man nothing to give his soul for the whole world...but for Wales?"

But for Wales? Or for an election? A position of power? Praise of the public? I say it simply isn't worth abandoning the content of your character.

Trying to please everyone by reacting or responding to their current opinion of you will ultimately run you and your business ragged. This principle is true about your role as a leader and in your personal life, as well.

So instead of swinging on the shifting sands of reputation, spend time today ensuring you are building your community, business, or organization based on character.

Lead your life, make hard decisions, and focus on the rock-solid principles at the heart of your character.

Evaluate your decision-making to see if there have been times you have allowed what others thought, or what they might have thought, to influence you. Decision-making is hard enough as it is; don't cloud the waters by trying to be a pleaser, as well.

It has been said that General Robert E. Lee was once asked his view of a man he had had many public disagreements with. Lee reportedly responded that the man was a good, just man whom he happened to disagree with greatly. The questioner then stated that the man in question did not hold such a respectful view of the general and often expressed that negative opinion to others publicly. To which General Lee replied, "You asked me my opinion of him, not my view of his view of me. My view is the only one over which I have control."

The way you communicate with those you disagree with speaks volumes about who you are as a person. Petty, personal attacks never produce positive results and often keep us a safe distance from real solutions.

Senator Orrin G. Hatch, a Republican from Utah, served in the United States Senate for forty-two years. He passed away April 23, 2022. Senator Hatch took me under his wing from the beginning. He helped on my campaigns, provided wise counsel on a host of issues, and encouraged me to raise my voice.

Senator Hatch was famous for his political odd-couple connection with Senator Ted Kennedy, a Democrat from Massachusetts. The conservative and the liberal disagreed on many things *and yet* they still came together to accomplish important work. They also took the time to develop a real friendship. I admired that.

I can't even count how many times Senator Hatch would pull me aside, compliment my work and efforts, provide some advice, or challenge me to take action on an issue.

It was in one of those conversations that Senator Hatch first encouraged me to join the Congressional Black Caucus. I must have looked unsure as he patted me on the shoulder and said, "I know you will be the only Republican in there and some Democrats will question your motives. I know some Republicans will call you a traitor and a sell-out. Do it anyway!"

I will be forever thankful that I took that advice; it changed my life and helped fortify my character and my focus on character as a member of Congress.

My husband, Jason, and I knew it was going to be crucial to be around people we could trust and who would have my back. Representative John Ratcliffe, a Republican from Texas, lived in the same building as I did, and he was just such a colleague and friend. John didn't want me running by myself in the morning. So, he would run with me. And we would make these runs around the National Mall, and we would talk about all sorts of things from freedom to family. It was simply a safe space in the midst of the chaos.

People like Tim Scott, Trey Gowdy, Mark Walker, John Ratcliffe, and Paul Ryan created the ultimate in safety for me. These colleagues, and some others, became the part of Washington that I loved. These people kept me sane. Some members would go out and have really hard nights. I don't drink but still wanted to connect with colleagues and avoid too much isolation. I knew I could always hang out with this group and that they would have my back.

This group always knew when to walk out of a room. When other colleagues began acting crazy or unruly, they would politely say that it was time to go. And they wouldn't just leave themselves. They would grab me by the elbow and say, "I think it's time to go."

My husband and I will forever be grateful. Because you don't know what you don't know in DC. I remember there was one point where Tim Scott said, "So if anything goes down here, which there is great potential for, we don't want to be anywhere around it. So, Mrs. Love, you're coming with us."

I had the members of the Utah delegation on my side as well. I went to Mike Lee and Orrin Hatch for very different things, but they both were always really good to me. Mike helped me stay grounded in principles and remain focused on good policy. As mentioned before, Orrin helped me with great advice and connections.

I do remember the first day that I got to Washington, Senator Hatch summoned me to his office. He sent a note through a staffer for me to go and visit him, which I did. Orrin looked at me, and said he had some advice for me. He began, "Mia, you look great. You look amazing. Don't go messing that up."

I said, "Excuse me, Senator? Don't go messing that up? What do you mean?"

The Senator responded, "A lot of people come here, their first year, they get depressed, they start eating a lot. You keep doing what you're doing. Stay fit. Run. It'll keep you here in a better mental state for a lot longer. Don't mess that up. You look great."

I took note and said, "Thank you, sir. Thank you." Some might have taken offense. It was endearing to me. Because one, I knew that this person wasn't mincing words. And I appreciate when somebody tells me exactly what they're feeling when they're feeling it. There is some comfort in that for me. Also, I could clearly see the benefits of staying healthy.

I remember meeting Senator Lee for the first time. It was in the basement of the Utah State Capitol after I had won the nomination in my first race. As you might expect, our conversation drifted toward the proper role of government. I finally said to him, "Senator, if I can make myself less powerful, and make people more powerful, I would have done my job. If I can put the decision-making into the hands of people, and not in my own, I would have done my job. If I can create more opportunities for the people that I serve, whether they were in my political party or not, I would have done my job."

Senator Lee responded. "We're all in! What do we need to do? How can I help you?" He helped me stay grounded in principles and remain focused on good policy.

Representative Rob Bishop, a Republican from Utah, also taught me a very important lesson. He had some pretty salty views on the Senate and its inability to get even good legislation through. He taught me to not let any senator think they were any better than a member of Congress. It was a little tongue in cheek, with his dry wit, but it was important for me to learn to function from a position of strength, not weakness—especially with members of the Senate.

There were countless others who always had my back, and I knew they were looking out for me.

Committee hearings might have been the source of my greatest frustration as a member of Congress. I am not sure they should even be called hearings because there are so many members who use their allotted time to pontificate and try to get their social media moment. I think my forehead became flat from the number of times I slapped my hand on my forehead and thought, "It just shouldn't be this hard." It is true; it shouldn't be this hard.

Norman Vincent Peale might have said it best: "We struggle with the complexities and avoid the simplicities."

Chasing the complex at the expense of the simple has become standard operating procedure in many organizations and government entities and congressional committees. It seems to be human nature for people to waste countless hours pursuing, exploring, evaluating, recreating, and ultimately discarding complex solutions to problems or opportunities when a simple solution could have done the job.

The last thing the world needs is another blue-ribbon committee to take something simple and transform it into something complex. Often it gets so complicated it becomes unactionable. There are countless "committee findings," reports, and recommendations stuffed in drawers and in the archives of the *Congressional Record*.

Simplicity was one of the things I loved most about being a mayor. Complexity was one of the most frustrating components of being a member of Congress.

Politics is forever chasing the complexities of the perfect solution for whatever the issue of the day might be.

It is as if health care, immigration, infrastructure, jobs, the economy, addiction, the climate, and a million other problems are all just one new program away from being solved. This has led some to think that if the government would only create a Happiness Agency all would be well with every American.

In all my running around the United States Capitol, in all my chasing to meetings, committee hearings, interviews, constituent meetings, and media appearances, I have never found a piece of policy or a government program that would create and foster such happiness.

In the late 1800s, an unknown author penned a set of principles titled "The Road to Happiness." The years have flown, the centuries have turned, times have changed, and technology has transformed the world—yet the road to real happiness remains unchanged.

Consider the principles in "The Road to Happiness":[4]

- Keep skid-chains on your tongue; always say less than you think. How you say things often counts far more than what you say.
- Make promises sparingly and keep them faithfully, no matter what it costs you.
- Never let an opportunity pass to say a kind and encouraging thing to or about somebody. Praise good work done, regardless of who did it. If

criticism is merited, criticize helpfully and never spitefully.

- Be interested in others: interested in their pursuits, their welfare, their homes, and families. Make merry with those who rejoice and mourn with those who weep. Let everyone you meet, however humble, feel that you regard them as a person of importance.
- Be cheerful. Keep the corners of your mouth turned up. Laugh at good stories and learn to tell them.
- Preserve an open mind on all debatable questions. Discuss, but don't argue. It is the mark of a superior mind to disagree and yet be friendly.
- Let your virtues, if you have any, speak for themselves, and refuse to talk of another's vices. Discourage gossip. Make it a point to say nothing to another unless it is something good.
- Be careful of others' feelings. Wit at the other fellow's expense is rarely worth the effort and may hurt where least expected.
- Pay no attention to ill-natured remarks about you. Simply live so that nobody will believe them.
- Don't be too anxious about getting your just dues. Do your work, be patient, keep your disposition sweet, forget self, and you will be respected and rewarded—on the road to Happiness!

Qualified

Remember that in the end, your character is who you really are and who you will be, based on what you have actually done rather than on what others think. Identify the core of your character and what it is that makes you who you truly are today—then live by it.

CHAPTER 10

What Might Have Been

I always felt throughout my life that I needed to be a voice for the voiceless, for the underrepresented, the underdog. Often I manifested this by speaking up for minority issues. Sometimes it was by trying to get my colleagues to reconsider long-held party politics and positions.

I have delivered countless speeches over the years in front of large crowds, on the floor of the House of Representatives, in front of a group of visiting grade-school children in my office, in committee hearings, at town halls, at conventions, at rallies, in churches, and more. I always felt a great responsibility when I was handed a microphone or placed in front of an audience.

The feeling of responsibility always takes me back to the Republican Convention in 2012. I am back in that bathroom stall, praying to be a voice, trying not to throw up. I find myself again pleading that the speech not be about me, but that it reflect the voices of those who will be listening. Praying that I could make a difference for someone.

In 2017, after winning the Marilyn Musgrave Defender of Life Award, I was called and asked to be one of the main speakers for the March for Life event on the National Mall. It was an opportunity to give voice to the truly voiceless—the yet-to-be-born. I felt an overwhelming responsibility to get this speech right. It mattered to me and to so many others.

It was a cold January day, but the crowd was warm and prepared to listen differently. The National Mall sometimes takes my breath away with all the history it contains, the heroes and heroines it honors, and the principles of freedom it enshrines.

I was thrilled to have my children and Jason with me on the stage. On this day, rather than having my back to Lincoln and facing the Capitol, I was facing Lincoln, and my words were heading toward the spot where Dr. King sent forth his booming words about being judged by the content of our character.

I prayed my words and voice would match the moment. My emotions were stirred in a way I hadn't ever experienced in front of a crowd—not even going back to my musical theater days. It was emotion, raw, real, and soul-connecting.

It is important to note that another march was going on simultaneously. That was the Women's March, which was primarily about women's reproductive rights. But that march was missing one very important thing: It was missing the voices of the most vulnerable among us—the yet-to-be-born.

I remember thinking out loud, "If I am not here serving these small and defenseless little ones, what's the point of having a voice on the national stage at all?" I had to stand up and speak out for those who couldn't vote, the ones who didn't have an audible voice, the ones who want so desperately to live. I firmly believe that.

My thoughts went to my parents and their American journey. In every moment that has mattered in my life and career, thoughts of my parents, their sacrifice, their grit, their determination, their willingness to do hard things, have been front and center in my mind. It all weighed mightily on my heart.

Preparing this speech was even more poignant in light of my parents' story, including my own beginning. I tried to imagine how they must have felt when they learned they were expecting me. The timing was surely subop-timal, with all the challenges they faced in their new country and with their two young children still in Haiti.

Having another mouth to feed was not going to make life easier. My parents were each working multiple jobs just to make ends meet. How could they keep that up with a new baby to take care of? If my mom were to quit even one of her jobs, the dollars and cents just wouldn't be enough, and the "making ends meet" couldn't possibly continue. Without all their jobs, they would most definitely run out of money before they could meet their monthly expenses. Adding me to the mix would also make it more difficult for my parents to see the path to bring my siblings to America to join them.

They had options. Hard, gut-wrenching options. But they had options. I always marvel that my mother and father chose life. They chose me. They chose the hard road and the more difficult path. In my preparation for the March for Life speech, I felt especially close to my parents and knew that in their example, I came to be. In their choices my voice was created. In their sacrifice my service to my country and my community became a possibility. In their willingness to see beyond the difficulty of their circumstances and envision the possibility of me in their lives, my opportunity to speak for the yet-to-be-born began.

Before going to the National Mall for the March for Life and my speech, I was in our hotel room getting ready. I had my children with me. We were staying in a corner suite, which gave us a unique perspective looking down into the streets. As we looked down, I could tell that our hotel was surrounded by protestors who were part of the Women's March. They were at the hotel protesting against Republicans. This was the site for the GOP political retreat that same weekend.

As my kids looked down at what was an increasingly angry protest and demonstration, my kids asked, "What are they protesting?" I replied that some of the people down in the street were part of the Women's March. I then explained to my kids, in ways that I thought would help them to think for themselves, the basis for their protest and the problem they had with those who believed differently about when life begins and whose life it is. I was very careful not to put any ideas in their minds but just create space for them to begin to learn for themselves. My kids' immediate response was, "Are you serious?"

We then had a discussion about the difference between being pro-life or pro-choice. I shared that such a choice wasn't as cut-and-dried as we would sometimes like to think. It was about a woman being able to make a decision between keeping a life and being alive. My kids could understand choices. What they couldn't understand was the anger, rage, and contempt that seemed to fill those who were participating in the Women's March.

I stressed that it was vital to recognize that it wasn't just the decision after becoming pregnant that mattered, but that I felt that women, young women in particular, should have more choices *before* that most difficult choice between preserving a life and expending a life. Too many women are not given the opportunity to have the choice before. I have long felt that women—again, young women in particular—should be able to have as many options before they have to make the choice between keeping a life or ending a life.

And then said to my kids, "You know, I am going to be speaking today at another march, and that's the March for Life." I continued, "You don't have to be there. There will be a lot of people, and I don't know what it's going to look like. But I'm speaking from the stage."

Having dragged my kids to a lot of events in their young lives, I felt like on this day, with this event and this speech, that they needed to choose whether they went or whether they stayed at the hotel.

When we travel together as a family, it is often a bit of organized chaos. Our hotel rooms often look like disaster areas with the kids' clothes and towels and back-packs, school supplies, snacks, and more scattered to the four corners of the rooms. As I looked at our life in that moment, I had a deep sense of gratitude for Jason and for each of our children.

I couldn't imagine our life without all of them. They each bring me joy in such different ways. Their unique gifts, talents, quirks, and personality traits make us a whole family. We learn from each other. We learn through each other. We most definitely test each other. Yes, we have our moments, as every family does, and through it all we draw closer together. We share a deep belief that families can be together forever. That hope drives our days.

On that day in that moment in that messy hotel room, I suddenly felt even closer to my kids. I drew great strength from their lives and their future possibilities. I wanted them to be with me and Jason on the stage in a way I hadn't felt previously. My children are part of me, an extension of me, and together with Jason, they make me whole.

I was about to ask again if they would rather go with us or stay at the hotel for the afternoon. Before I could say another word, they all said they wanted to go to the march and attend the event. Then they asked, "Can we stand up on the stage with you when you give your speech?"

They all wanted to stand up there. They didn't just want to be down in the crowd. They felt compelled to truly stand up and be part of my support on the stage. For them, that march on that day was their protest. That was their march. They wanted to stand up for something. They wanted to be part of something bigger than themselves—something that mattered and something that could make a difference. They recognized I was raising my voice for the voiceless and that by standing with me they could, in their own way, help the helpless.

In the end my kids didn't care about the rush of being up on the stage or the cheering crowd on the National

Mall. The moment became a personal moment that mattered for my children.

I had worked extensively with Boyd Matheson on the speech. Then in my final preparations, I gave the speech to Lee Zeldin, my friend and a Republican congressman from New York, to get a sense if the message could truly match the moment. Lee was someone who I could always bounce ideas off of, and I knew that he would give honest feedback and input.

I was a little hesitant to actually read the speech to him, knowing that it might not be his kind of speech. But I somehow knew I needed him to hear it. I delivered it to him and then waited in that uncomfortable silence for his reaction. I wanted him to at least like the speech.

Lee Zeldin said, "Wow, this is really good!" He continued, "Nothing touches me, and this is not just good. It is crazy good. You moved me. Yeah, Mia, you absolutely have to give that speech in that way." His response reinforced my confidence in the speech, the message, and my ability to deliver it.

I remember it was a bitterly cold day. I don't like being cold. But I had my kids behind me and a supportive crowd in front of me. I was ready to raise my voice for the voiceless.

I got up and spoke from the heart once again, no papers in front of me—just me and my message. I spoke about my life and living with my three children, who were standing close behind me. I spoke of those defining moments, those little hinges that turned my thoughts and transformed my soul and impacted me in a significant way.

It was incredibly meaningful for my kids to be there. It is one thing to say you believe something or support something. It's another thing to get out there and stand up together. I think my kids saw me a little differently that day. More important, they saw themselves a little differently that day. I think they also felt the power of gathering. Recognizing that there are other people that are willing to stand up with you and come out on a bitterly cold day, a day many could have said, "I will just watch from home," is empowering. Truly there isn't anything more encouraging than seeing that you're not alone.

Here is the text of my speech as prepared for delivery on Friday, January 27, 2017, in Washington, DC, on the National Mall as part of the March for Life:

Inside the womb and out—life has meaning, and that meaning matters.

Every child matters; every life at every stage makes a difference.

Some forty-one years ago a struggling couple arrived in America. They had left their faltering country, entrusted their two children—who they wouldn't see for five years—in the care of family members, and embarked for this land of opportunity.

It was inconvenient for them to find out they were going to have a third child while both had to work multiple jobs just to make ends meet. It would have been easier for them to have an abortion. This couple had a choice to make: protect the life of their child or always wonder what might have been.

John Greenleaf Whittier wrote, "Of all sad words of tongue or pen, the saddest are these: 'It might have been.'"

Each child, born and unborn, has the potential to open up our world and take us to places and spaces we haven't even imagined. Each living child carries with him or her the potential for greatness. A child born today may become the doctor that cures cancer or Alzheimer's. That child may become the astronaut that takes the world to Mars or the CEO that leads a global business. That child may become the friend who saves a peer from suicide or the mom that strengthens a family. That child may become the neighbor that unites a community, the volunteer who eradicates hunger, or the teacher who inspires a struggling student.

Every time we kill a child though abortion we kill potential. Every time we kill a child, we—all of us—suffer. We lose a little of ourselves and a lot of our future.

We strip a child from their God-given potential when we, as a society, accept abortion as "health care." We cannot accept what might have been.

We won't know what might have been when we allow organizations like Planned Parenthood to convince a pregnant woman that "they have no choice" but to abort the life and potential within them. We cannot accept what might have been.

We won't know what might have been when organizations limit women from being empowered so they can profit. Such organizations prefer women to be victims because they know that a truly empowered woman doesn't need their controlling influence. We cannot accept what might have been.

We won't know what might have been when we allow Planned Parenthood to convince our girls in the inner city that the only way they can be empowered to have a life is by choosing to end a life. We cannot accept what might have been.

Instead of listening to the haunting refrains of "what might have been," we must instead focus on what is and what is to come.

I love the line from Victor Hugo's *Les Mis*: "There is nothing like a dream to create the future." A life—born or yet to be born—is, and can create, a future filled with daring dreams.

During that other, angrier, "march on Washington" last week I saw a picture of a black teenage girl in the crowd who was holding a sign that said, "I survived *Roe v. Wade*—but it won't survive me!"

This young woman beat the odds and was born into a world that far too often favors the abortion of a black girl over the life of a black girl. She could have become part of "what might have been." But today she is a part of what is—and I can't wait to see what she and thousands just like her become in the years ahead.

Forty-one years ago, that couple from Haiti could have made the choice to abort. But they didn't. They chose life. They chose what was and what could be. They went forward to foster that life and the future and dreams that baby would bring. I am certain that this couple never could have conceived that that child would be elected to the United States House of Representatives as the very first Black Republican woman ever elected to Congress. But more than that, they would have never dreamed that that child would grow up to fight for all children, especially for those yet to be born.

We all have talents, gifts, purpose and potential to be used for the blessing of society. All we are asking is that we no longer settle for "what might have been" and instead embrace the possibilities of the life that is and is to come. The life of those born and yet to be born deserve the chance to dream and create their own future.

Thank you.

After the speech I went on CNN. It was a very positive interview and experience. There weren't any gotcha questions or angry talking points, because I had just spoken truth from my heart with my kids standing by me.

My kids have endured a lot of political events where they just had to wait around for mom, or eat that rubber chicken, or pretend they were happy to be there. I was so thankful that they wanted to be with me on that day and that we marched together. Having them with me on the journey that day reminded me of what I was doing and who I was fighting for. I knew the march, and my speech became more than just another political event; those moments were about my kids contemplating what kind of world they would grow up living in.

My kids saw their mom get up and be a warrior that day—not a mean warrior or an evil one. They saw that I could stand and raise my voice as a respectful warrior, a gentle warrior, but a warrior nonetheless.

On that very cold day, in front of that incredibly large crowd, in that most historic place, I came to understand truly what it means to own my story, raise my voice, and lead with character. It was an important moment in my progression and development, one that reminds me that being qualified isn't a destination or a set of skills or accomplishments.

Being qualified begins with recognizing that your infinite worth, and the worth of others, comes from within.

CHAPTER 11

Raising Dreamers and Leading Others

I was asked recently about my relationship with my mother and father. I am profoundly close to both. My admiration for my mother and all that she went through knows no bounds. My dad and I have always had a very special and close relationship.

I loved being around my dad. It was under his watchful eye and subtle influence that I gained an appreciation for freedom and learned of the fragility of American exceptionalism. I was speaking to a group of young people on one occasion and was about to share some of the priceless lessons my dad had taught me. During the conversation, someone asked, "Why your dad? What was it about your dad that made your relationship close and put you in a place to learn such lessons?"

As I began to answer the question, a memory that had been lost for decades popped into my mind.

As I have shared, my mother and father made the extraordinary sacrifice to leave their two older children in Haiti in order to get settled and started in America. My parents went five years without them before they had the status that would allow my brother and sister to come into the United States legally.

I had been born during that period in America and remember being an only child for my early years. I remember that my mom was so overjoyed when we went to pick my siblings up. Heading to the airport I am sure brought back many feelings of guilt for my mom for being separated from her two oldest children for so long.

I didn't understand what was happening. All I knew was that I had been the center of life for my mom and dad, and now two other children were crashing my party.

At the John F. Kennedy International Airport in New York, we found my siblings. I couldn't figure out why my parents were holding these two strangers so tightly and why they wouldn't let them go.

As we were walking to the car, I fell behind more and more as I attempted to make sense of my new situation. I must have been at least fifty feet behind my parents and newfound brother and sister.

It was my dad who stopped when he noticed I wasn't right there with them. He turned around, put my brother down, and ran back and picked me up. I don't remember him saying anything to me verbally, but I do remember the look and feeling I got in that most powerful moment. The look my dad gave me said, "You are not forgotten. I noticed you, I see you, and I won't ever let you go."

There is nothing more important for a child—or an adult—than to feel seen and known. *New York Times* writer David Brooks calls this "seeing each other deeply and being deeply seen."[1] It is one of the most powerful parenting and leadership principles anywhere.

My husband and I eventually brought three beautiful children into the world. Like my parents did, I have aspired to teach my children to dream improbable dreams and raise them up to know that they can do anything they set their minds to do. Through hard work and determination, real results can be achieved—but not through handouts, only hand-ups.

I was surprised at the family child-rearing questions that arose as I stepped onto the field of politics. Citizens, neighbors, and strangers alike would ask questions including, "Do you really want to place this political label on yourself, as well as your children?" and "Do you really feel it is necessary to raise your children to have and hold conservative ideals?" These questions were quickly put to rest by the strength of my beliefs and hopes for the future. I raise my kids to have their own beliefs and consider the issues around them. At my house, considering the issues isn't enough. We always have challenged our children to figure out what they want to do about any issue we discuss.

I hope your kids will do the same and that you empower them to see right, do right, and evaluate each situation.

Raising up the next generation to continue in our work for change, progress, justice, equality, and freedom is all our duty. With each generation I believe there is hope for improvement and advancement toward a place of unity, peace, and success.

While trying to help my own children live up to their potential, there were many days filled with a lot of "mom guilt." I remember a period when Alessa was on the swim team, and Abi was trying to figure out what she was doing with her sports future. She was playing basketball but had just torn her ACL for the first time and needed reconstructive surgery followed by a long road of rehabilitation. Peyton was a ball of energy, high on activity, and low on focusing on tasks and homework. There were things happening at a hectic pace in DC that preoccupied my mind, and I found myself wandering through day after day filled with guilt. All day. Every day. I didn't seem to be succeeding at anything—especially not when it came to teaching and strengthening and supporting my children, which is the worst of all the mom guilt.

Raising up the next generation of great Americans requires you to be willing to learn from them and be surprised by them. It is a fact that sometimes your kids are the ones who tell you exactly what you need to hear without your even asking.

I was on the floor of the House of Representatives in the Capitol one afternoon. I had just gotten through speaking with Alessa and helping her remember where her swim stuff was and what gear she needed to take with her to practice. Classic mom conversation. Classic child response once you remind them of the thing you had already told them a thousand times and that they had promised they would remember. I immediately started to project what would happen if she forgot again, what the coach would say. Surely, he would judge the mom who was three thousand miles away in Washington, DC. I could feel my guilt-o-meter rising.

Then my amazing daughter sent me a text message: "Mom, I'm really proud of you. You're doing some great things. And you're teaching me that I can be more than just a great person, a great mom, and a great wife. That I have talents I need to discover. Those talents that were given to me by God. So, thanks, Mom."

I lost it. I cried on the floor of the House. In addition to being thankful for kids who just got it, I also recognized that some of the lessons I have tried to teach my kids have come full circle; they have now taught them to me. That knowledge sweeps away a lot of guilt when I recognize what they have learned along the way.

There was one time when Alessa called me and she was really, really upset. She was in a religious seminary class at the high school, and she told me that the teacher was telling the guys in the class not to date girls if they were in college and focused on careers. "Don't take those girls out on dates," he said.

Alessa said to me, "Ma, he was pretty much telling these boys not to date me." I replied, "Well, he didn't say you." And she countered, "Well, I'm going to college. And I want to build rockets. You know, but I want to date, and I want to get married. I know how important that is."

We had dealt with misinformation before, and she knew that we could work through this. I had learned that she wasn't going to let it go, that she was going to address it and fix it—if not for herself, then for all of the other girls.

I went into the cloakroom, and I started looking up quotes by leaders of The Church of Jesus Christ of Latter-day Saints relating to women working and being educated. I immediately found one from Brigham Young dating all the way back to 1869. Young declared, "As I have often told my sisters in the Female Relief Societies, we have sisters here who, if they had the privilege of studying, would make just as good mathematicians or accountants as any man; and we think they ought to have the privilege to study these branches of knowledge that they may develop the powers with which they are endowed. We believe that women are useful, not only to sweep houses, wash dishes, make beds, and raise babies, but that they should stand behind the counter, study law or physic, or become good book-keepers and be able to do the business in any counting house, and all this to enlarge their sphere of usefulness for the benefit of society at large. In following these things they but answer the design of their creation. These and many more things of equal utility are incorporated in our religion, and we believe in and try to practice them."[2]

Alessa was so excited to learn that this quote came from a church leader in the 1860s, which was awesome to her. She shared that quote with her seminary teacher and the class. She said to the teacher, "You're telling these guys not to date these girls, when this is actually something that was said by a leader of the Church. Brigham Young was telling women to be educated and productive members of society. You should be educated on this."

Alessa and I took on this teacher—me from Washington, her from the classroom; we were not willing to back down.

We went on to find other quotes from church leaders

that answered the question, "Do we encourage education?" Of course, the answer, by all means, is that every young woman ought to be encouraged to refine her skills and increase her abilities to broaden her knowledge and strengthen her capacity. What a tragic thing it is to see a young woman become entrapped in practices that destroy her potential and cut short her divine destination.

The teacher asked my daughter for my email. She texted me, saying, Ma, he's asking for your email. I texted back, Did you say these things respectfully? She reassured me, saying, Mom, I'm always respectful.

The instructor did send me an email. He said that Alessa's interpretation was not at all what he meant, and he explained his side of it to me. Then he wrote, But I'm so grateful you have a strong daughter, that will set me straight sometimes and make sure I'm careful with my words, and mindful of what I portray, and what I'm telling the students. That's an awesome thing.

That lesson came from Washington, and it came from her having the courage to stand up when she needed to, to not stay silent, to speak up. I see a lot of parents whose first instinct is to take their kids out of the classroom rather than lean into opportunities to work with teachers and administrators to foster better teachers and encourage better learning. My job as a mother, as a wife, and as a member of Congress is to teach. Often that teaching is done through showing or setting an example.

I think it is vital for every kid to be able to look at seemingly impossible things and say, "I can do that." Our job is to help them do that. We don't tell them to leave the classroom; we give them information so that they can make an informed argument and maybe learn something. At my house, we don't run away.

If I ran away and didn't become a member of the Congressional Black Caucus, I wouldn't have been able to be influenced or have influence. Leaders put themselves in uncomfortable positions and learn to get comfortable there. Then they move on to the next uncomfortable thing. Leaders get comfortable having uncomfortable conversations, and that goes for everything. That's what leaders do.

And when I run on the treadmill, I have notes filled with a lot of motivational sayings or things that inspire me or cause me to think differently. I say, "Today, I'm doing this." One of my favorites over the years that I have tried to pass on to the dreamers and future leaders in my home says, "Today, be willing to do what most people won't so that tomorrow you can do what most people can't."

I have other sayings, like, "If you feel like crap today, it's just so you can feel much better about doing this tomorrow." Or things like, "Imagine how great it's going to feel when you're done."

You can't really appreciate how good you feel when

you're done if that's how you feel all the time. It's the uncomfortable that's going to get you stronger and make you better. I share that it's the exercise with resistance that builds the muscle in you and obstacles are the way to stronger self.

Principles of leadership are important to recognize, celebrate, and emulate. Raising the next generation is hard work and requires precision, not generalized teaching and leading.

One of the driving forces of my belief in limited government, federalism, and local control has actually been my children. I have seen what happens when one-size-fits-all curriculum or mandates are handed down from the federal government. I have also seen the power of parents when they work with teachers and local administrators to meet and adapt to the needs of individual students.

Local control isn't just about making the federal government smaller or saving tax dollars. Local control is where the uniqueness of each student can be recognized, valued, and improved. Federal mandates are tailored to the masses—and often play to stereotypes, classes, and the mediocre middle that can be easily managed and measured. That approach drove me crazy as a mother and as a lawmaker!

In a TED Talk about his book *The End of Average*,[3] author Todd Rose looked at the reasons why an assembly-line-style education system was failing American students. Rose used as his premise an example from the U.S. Air Force in the 1950s. Crashes and poor pilot performance were devastating the organization. After blaming pilots, instructors, and commanders, a team of researchers eventually began to look at the design of the cockpits.

Cockpits were being created to the average size of a typical Air Force pilot based on ten physical dimensions. More than four thousand airmen had their measurements taken and logged. Everyone seemed to be convinced that such calculations, producing the "average pilot," would transform cockpit efficiencies, reduce crashes, and improve performance.

To the surprise of most on the research team, out of the more than four thousand pilots measured, not a single one fit the average on all ten dimensions. Some pilots were tall in height but had shorter arms, and others had bigger chests but shorter legs. The big discovery was that there really was no such thing as an average pilot. In designing a cockpit to fit the average pilot, they were actually designing it to fit no one at all.

Rose concluded that mass-producing education for the masses doesn't really work because there is no average student—*ever*!

Think about that as a parent: In designing education to the average student, big government is educating no one at all. I am so thankful to those dedicated teachers who have worked tirelessly to educate to the uniqueness of each of my children.

The most important skill for raising dreamers is teaching them to think. Staying fearlessly curious is so crucial. Sadly, far too many public schools are set up to teach children everything except how to use their own minds, think independently, and stay curious.

Lack of curiosity is a real, clear, and present danger to our country. One of the things I love about being on CNN is that I am constantly challenged to stay curious.

My path to CNN actually began with Trey Gowdy, who set me up with his agent, Olivia Metzger. She's a fireball who reminded me of a woman who actually did my fund-raising, Paige Marriott. We hit it off. Olivia set me up with just a couple of meetings so I could get to know a couple of people at CNN. I remember sitting down in a meeting with a woman named Rebecca Cutler. We talked about our families. We talked about everything but politics.

Finally, I asked her a question. I wondered if CNN was going to be okay with my being a conservative. She replied that they would be more than okay with any authentic thought that I honestly have experienced or felt was in bounds. I would be protected.

I felt good about that. CNN is a place where we don't have to advocate and echo just one voice—that I can add my unique voice and point of view. My hope is always that maybe someone out there watching will look and say, "Hmm, that makes sense."

I am so glad to be part of CNN. My philosophy has always been to go to places that are uncomfortable and get comfortable. That's where leaders are born and made. It is difficult to make a difference when you're preaching to the choir. When everybody you're talking with or to are in an echo chamber, and everybody's saying the same thing, there is little substance or value.

You can only make a difference when you're able to offer a different perspective, opinion, or point of view. And I'm glad I landed at CNN in the same way that I'm glad that I joined the Congressional Black Caucus. You get into an occasional heated debate. I'm okay with that. Debate is good.

CNN host Jake Tapper surprised me the most because I hadn't anticipated going in that we would go beyond colleagues to become real, authentic friends. When my Republican colleagues or former colleagues prepare to go on Jake's show, I tell them that the only thing that you cannot do with Jake is lie. Do not make anything up. Because not only will Jake catch you, he will be offended that you lied to him more than he is upset with the content. The truth matters to Jake—and I love that.

Erin Burnett is like a rock star. She is living the life—having children and kicking butt as an anchor. I mean, she just she doesn't miss a beat. I have learned so much from her.

Wolf Blitzer, I have to say, is my mom's favorite. For me, Wolf was my very first interview following my big speech at the Republican Convention in Tampa. Wolf is endearing. He's always reminding me, "This is prime time. This is big stuff. You know, we're big. We're a big deal. You ready?" I always respond by reminding Wolf that this is a bigger deal because my mom is watching you right now. To which Wolf replies, "Oh, tell your mother I love her."

CNN keeps me curious. Far too many in this country have become so insulated in their own news feeds or social media bubbles that they have lost their curiosity. They lost the capacity to even consider, "I wonder why she thinks that way?" or "Why would he believe that is the best way to solve that problem?"

I have learned so much from my colleagues at CNN who think differently than I do.

Sadly, when we lose our curiosity, the divisions in our homes and communities grow deeper. When we lack curiosity, which also nurtures humility, we tend to hunker down when given information or insight regarding a particular issue. We react when our thinking gets challenged by another point of view, so we resort to instant certainty about our own opinion. We become more certain, so we don't even have to listen to anyone else.

Curiosity may have killed the cat, but I believe it can save the country.

Raising children is a challenge. So is helping those you lead learn to lead themselves.

Self-leadership begins with taking responsibility, refusing to be a victim, and avoiding becoming bitter. No finger pointing. No shrugging shoulders. No placing blame. Personal responsibility is vital.

In his novel *The Light Between Oceans*, M. L. Stedman captures a conversation between a man who had been abused and mistreated by the people of the town and his wife, who could not understand his warmhearted forgiveness and his absolute rejection of any feelings of contempt toward the townspeople.

When his wife asked how he could show such forgiveness, the man replied, "I choose to. I can leave myself to rot in the past, spend my time hating people for what happened...or I can forgive and forget."

"But it's not that easy," she answered.

He smiled and said, "Oh, but...it is so much less exhausting. You only have to forgive once. To resent, you have to do it all day, every day. You have to keep remembering all the bad things."[4]

Becoming bitter requires a lot of work. Going around looking for reasons to be offended is bad for the soul. Forgiveness is freeing. There were so many things in Washington that I could have held a grudge about, but it would have prevented me from solving real problems and getting things done.

We have to be able to make decisions and live with the consequences no matter how brilliant or how flawed we are.

Whether you are raising your children or leading a team or contributing to your community, there are seven things that everyone needs to know and keep in mind. I often share these principles with young people on college campuses. They apply everywhere.

- **Purpose.** Choose a purpose, a grand aspiration, or a big goal, and move toward it relentlessly.
- **Mastery over self.** Discipline equals freedom. If you're driven by impulse all your life, you will drift and go nowhere in the end.
- **Learning from adversity.** Failures are just failures. Failures should never define you, and they will refine you, and make you better if you stop and learn from them.
- **Be a light.** You must be confident enough to have rational, respectful conversations with people you don't agree with. You can't light a flame if you are too afraid to think for yourself. We have to get comfortable in uncomfortable situations.
- **Time.** Time can make drifting and negativity permanent. We all get twenty-four hours in a day—

no more and no less. What we choose to do with that time is what will define us in the end.

- **Harmony.** In order for you to balance the mental, spiritual, and physical aspects of your life, you must be the author of your life. It is up to you to create the balance.
- **Caution.** Always act. *And*—always think before you act. You need both caution and action.

I am so thankful for my parents—especially my dad, who helped me gain confidence in myself by helping me know what he saw in me.

Since leaving Congress I have been committed to lending my voice to principled organizations and causes, especially those focused on developing young people. Becoming a national outreach director and mentor for the Center for Growth and Opportunity (CGO) at Utah State University has been a perfect fit. I love the vision of student-led, nonpartisan, research-discovering solutions to the biggest challenges of our day. The work of CGO and the student researchers gives me great hope for the future of America.

Raising dreamers and helping others learn to be leaders themselves is really the test for all of us. Such a commitment to raise and lead changes children, transforms communities, and empowers nations.

CHAPTER 12

The Future of Principles over Politics

O ver the course of my political career, the question I get asked most changed from "How could you be a Republican?" to "How can I remain in the party of Donald Trump?" There were many versions and itera- tions of these questions over the years. Those who asked such questions clearly didn't understand who I am, why I was in office, or what I actually believe.

For me, this journey was never about a political party or any politician; for me, the answers to these questions are always found in the principles I had experienced for myself and come to hold as part of the content of my character.

"Yeah, but..." If I got a nickel for every conversation I had with a hostile constituent, berating reporter, or angry social media troll that included the phrase, "Yeah, but...," I would be a millionaire.

The conversation would usually start with a principle and then move to a policy. As it should. Then, if they thought they were losing an argument and had to agree to common ground, they would throw out some version of "Yeah, but the Republicans are evil because they..." or "Yeah, that is true, but President Trump is..."

When we anchor ourselves to a political party or to a political figure, we are doomed. Parties and personalities don't own principles or even policies. I firmly believe that politicians rarely lead America. Culture, communities, and principles lead, and the politicians usually follow. I was amazed during my time in Congress at how good politicians were at running to the front of a parade and acting as if they had led it from the beginning.

The questions for me about my membership in the GOP became sharper toward the end of my time in Congress—particularly after President Trump insulted my ancestral home and threw a personal dig at my narrow reelection loss in 2018.

My quick comeback to such questions has always been

that I've been a Republican longer than the forty-fifth president has. The more accurate response to those questions is the same today as it had always been: I will never abandon my ideals and principles because of a party affiliation or a name on the ballot.

I am astonished at how many of my peers and dyed-in-the-wool Republicans would distance themselves from proven conservative policies and ideas in their attempts to take a step away from behavior they found unseemly in Donald Trump. The president isn't the center of the party—at least no president ever should be. A president, in my view, should be just one of many leaders in a party. The principles should be the middle of the middle, followed by policies, and then the people who believe in them, and then the transitory leaders who occupy positions of power for a season.

I always looked to George Washington as the model of recognizing that every politician can, and regularly should, be replaced. One of my favorite parts of the Capitol is the rotunda. I admit I loved to walk into the Capitol rotunda and look at the statues and murals. One of the most stunning murals depicts General Washington as he resigns his commission.

December 23, 1783, is a day worth noting, remembering, and studying. On that day, in the ultimate act of servant-leadership, General George Washington resigned his commission before the Continental Congress. In one of the few instances in history, the commander of the conquering forces did not assume complete authority, control, and power, but instead returned them to the citizens and their representatives.

George Washington clearly understood that power is not something to amass, barter with, or cling to, nor is it a tool for pursuing political purposes and self-promotion. While many proclaimed him to be indispensable and irreplaceable, Washington knew that the future of the nation wasn't dependent on him. He believed America's destiny would be secured down through the ages by individual citizens who would enter the world's stage and make contributions in their homes, communities, and country before traveling on.

I believed that when I was in elected office, and I believe it even more today.

In January 2018, President Trump had a number of members of Congress in the Oval Office for a meeting on immigration reform. In what I regard as a moment more revealing of his character than anything else, he asked those in the room, "Why do we want all these people from shithole countries coming here?"

Senator Dick Durbin, the Democratic minority whip at the time, was explaining to the president a proposal to end the visa lottery in exchange for Temporary Protected Status (TPS) for countries such as El Salvador. Durbin was going through a list of TPS countries that would be covered. When he got to Haiti, Trump asked why the United States would want more people from Haiti and African countries.

The comment shocked those in the room and sent shock waves through social media and cable news outlets. It was one more disappointing moment for me and the Party of Lincoln.

As the first Haitian-American elected to Congress, everyone immediately wanted to know what my thoughts and reaction were.

I said at the time that President Trump's comments were unkind, divisive, elitist, and flew in the face of our nation's values. I called on the president to apologize to both the American people and the nations he so wantonly maligned.

I went on to share my parents' story. Not just where they were born, but what they sacrificed because of their belief in the goodness of America. I described how they came from one of those countries the president derided, but proudly took an oath of allegiance to the United States and took on the responsibilities of everything that being a citizen entails. They never took a thing from our federal government. They worked hard, paid taxes, and rose from nothing to take care of and provide opportunities for their children. They taught their children to do the same. That's the American Dream.

I obviously knew what the American Dream was because I was living it.

That was a disappointing day in my Washington experience in many ways. It was doubly disappointing because my dad was also deeply disappointed in the president's comments. My dad had been supportive and encouraged by many of the policies that were moving forward under the Trump administration. I sensed the disconnect driven by contemptuous words and the wedge it could have created between my dad and the country he chose to make his own. And yet, Trump's arrogant and insensitive words also reenforced my belief that the founder of our nation understood that it would be possible for people to obtain office, even the highest office, and still have significant character flaws, blind spots, arrogance, and elitist attitudes. And the nation can still survive through checks and balances and the American people raising their voices at the voting booth.

When it comes to the direction of the country, we should always remember that the executive branch is balanced by the Supreme Court and 535 elected leaders in Congress.

I believe it is one more example of the political false choice: that a citizen or elected official would be forced to pick between supporting a president or defending his or her ideals.

As the 2018 election cycle ramped up, I found myself

facing Democrat Ben McAdams, who was the Salt Lake County mayor at the time. He appeared to be a nice guy. The contrast between the "regular nice guy" and the lies told and aspersions cast by a relentless attack on my character caused me to question if he was just comfortable winning at any cost or a wolf in sheep's clothing.

It was another brutal campaign. Once again, the race was too close to call, and the final results didn't come in on election night. Of course, that didn't stop an angry President Trump from weighing in the next morning with a jab at me for not using him more during the campaign.

"Mia Love gave me no love, and she lost," Trump said. "Too bad. Sorry about that, Mia."[1]

The president talked about how I would call and ask for his help with Josh Holt, a Utahn who was being held in prison by the Venezuelan government. The president was clearly trying to justify losses and reframe his importance.

The president's behavior toward me made me wonder: What did he have to gain by saying such a thing about a fellow Republican? It was not really about asking him to do more, was it? Or was it something else?

In the end, I had lost to McAdams by fewer than seven hundred votes. The margin was just outside the range where a recount would have happened. The difference turned out to be Salt Lake County, where a marijuana initiative on the ballot pushed many more young, non-off-year liberal voters to the polls.

It was hard to come that close again and end up short. But I was at peace knowing that I had never sold my soul for a vote or a short-term victory.

In my concession speech, I addressed President Trump's comments and the future of the Republican Party. I said that the president's remarks gave me a clear vision of his world as it was—no real relationships, just convenient transactions. That was an insufficient way to implement sincere service and policies.

I shifted my attention to the larger problem Republicans in Washington have with minority voters. I said in my remarks, "This election experience and these comments shine a spotlight on the problems Washington politicians have with minorities and black Americans—it's transactional, it's not personal."

I tried to help Republicans understand how the minority communities saw them. "You see, we feel like politicians claim they know what's best for us from a safe distance, yet they're never willing to take us home. Because Republicans never take minority communities into their home and citizens into their hearts, they stay with Democrats and bureaucrats in Washington because at least they make them feel like they have a home—or at least make them feel valued."

There is an opportunity for a different kind of

conversation with minority communities. Many are realizing that the government's promises of providing exactly what you need to stay exactly where you are currently are hollow.

The thought that kept running through my mind in the days following my loss was a quote that has long been wrongly attributed to Winston Churchill, but rings true to me regardless of its origin: "Success is not final, failure is not fatal: it is the courage to continue that counts."

Regardless of who did, didn't, or might have said something like it, I had lived the principles. And I now had an opportunity to explore if I had the courage to continue and discover what was next for my family and my voice.

In my speech I challenged the status quo, saying, "Minority communities need to ask themselves a question also: 'What is the cost of staying with the Democrat party that perpetually delivers exactly what you need to stay exactly where you are?'

"I am a Republican. I know conservative policies work. They lift everyone, they lift the poor, the young, the vulnerable, the black and the white."

My message about conservative principles is the same today, though my truth runs deeper. I know a little more about failure, and I know more about how this government works and the individual dynamics of the people now in charge. I am unleashed, untethered, and unshackled from an official role in the Republican Party. And I will say exactly what's on my mind.

I continue to share my story and hope to be a voice, an image, and a leader that inspires others to follow in my footsteps. I am still advocating my principles boldly as a commentator on CNN platforms.

Don't worry—I know that I am usually the token conservative or Republican on a panel. I also know that my voice can break through the chatter and help people from both political parties see critical issues in different ways. I have been treated with great respect by my colleagues at CNN, and I love the conversations we have that produce elevated dialogue about not just the news of the day, but the future of the country.

Though my political party doesn't always communicate how it supports immigration, I regularly call the GOP out for not living up to principles and policies they should embrace and drive. Because of my story and my parents' stories, I have a deep connection to the realities of immigration and speak out on it regularly.

As a hot topic right now, I passionately believe that Republicans should be embracing immigrants. Studies continually show that if we follow the Constitution and create a uniform rule of naturalization, the economic benefits of having a welcoming immigration policy can only be good for the United States.

There are people who believe they just want highly

skilled workers coming into the United States. They want high-tech, they want engineers, they want brain surgeons. But what about the people like my mother? She worked in a nursing home upon arrival in America to take care of the elderly. Not only did she provide a necessary honorable service, but she also began paying into entitlement programs right away, directly stimulating the economy.

Immigrants like my mom begin paying taxes, paying into Medicare, paying into Social Security. On the other hand, high-skilled workers are most likely still going to school. It takes them ten to twelve years before they're actually paying into these systems. There is a purely economic argument to be made, and that is just the beginning. We are all Americans through immigrant lineage; it only makes sense that we would embrace good immigration policy.

Even if you looked at immigration as a purely political issue, it still makes sense for Republicans to engage in immigration conversations in the Hispanic and Latino communities. These communities are entrepreneurial, family centered, hardworking, and highly engaged in faith-based organizations. Sounds pretty conservative to me! Of course, no community is monolithic in its politics, but it is true that if you don't show up, you can't have a conversation or a connection. Without a connection, there is no future.

I often revert back to telling my family's story in this simple way to teach the principle over the politics:

Two people immigrated to America from Haiti with just $10 in their pockets and the hope that America really did exist and could provide opportunity. They were willing to work really hard. As a long-term result of their immigration, they had a daughter who became the first and only Black female Republican ever elected to the United States Congress. That service directly impacted policies and made a difference for the good of all citizens. That drove generational change. My parents came from a third world country, began working and paying right away into American systems, and produced children that contribute to society and are able to help others. If that is not an American story, I don't know what is.

One thing I never tired of during my days in DC was seeing the sun rise in the sky while running past a historic monument. The rising sun is both inspiring and instructive for us today as we face significant national and international challenges.

Looking back over our history as a nation, we can see America's beginning was anything but certain, and we faced daunting difficulties not dissimilar from what we face today. As the last delegates were signing the historic and inspired document we revere as the Constitution, Benjamin Franklin pointed toward the sun on the back of the Convention president's chair. Then he made a most important observation, as only he could, saying, *"I have often looked at that picture behind the president without being able to tell whether it was rising or setting. But now at length I have the happiness to know that it is a rising and not a setting sun."*[2]

From that moment until today, America has been on the rise—and I am convinced that the best is yet to come. The great American rising has always been based on our belief in the ability of every individual to rise like the morning sun. That belief in *all* people is what makes us different here in Utah and what is at the heart of the Republican Party.

My friend Arthur Brooks often shared with me what he believed was the difference between liberals and conservatives by saying something like: "Liberals believe that the poor and the needy are liabilities to be managed. Conservatives believe the poor are human assets, with unlimited potential to rise, that need to be nurtured."

That is my vision of the future for principles over politics. I believe that given the opportunity, the American people will always rise to the occasion—on their own. No nanny state needed, no big-government mandate required. We are Americans!

For more than two hundred years, when given the opportunity, we have lent a hand and lifted the poor. Given the opportunity, we have pulled ourselves up and united to put down tyranny and evil. Given the opportunity, we overcome overwhelming odds, drive innovative ideas, and achieve the seemingly impossible. Given the opportunity, we Americans rally for good causes whether they are down the street, across town, or around the world.

Unfortunately, many in Washington on both sides of the political aisle don't trust the American people. Washington doesn't seem to want us to have those opportunities to rise to the occasion. Just "trust Washington," they say, "trust Washington to take care of everything"—to raise our children, control our lands, and dictate every aspect of our lives.

I have sat through some interesting hearings and committee meetings during my time in Congress. One day, I sat in disbelief when one of my colleagues was pointing at a map of the poorest cities in America, touting how Democrats were the champions of the poor—because the cities with the most poverty were all run by or represented in Congress by Democrats!

I remember sitting there thinking, "Oh no, she didn't!" I was stunned. I tried to stay quiet—I really did—but finally I had to say something. I pointed to the map and said, "That map is an indictment of your policies. Your policies are not giving the poor the opportunity to rise!"

Instead of looking to Washington, we need to help people look within. I think it is high time for Washington to trust the American people.

For example, imagine a health care system that is

centered in service and measured by outcome—not dictated by Washington. Given the opportunity, I see American exceptionalism rising to the occasion to create a health care system where innovation, compassion, and people drive the highest quality care.

Imagine a single mother who is trapped in poverty by big-government programs that prevent her from taking new opportunities and proving that she can rise to the occasion. I believe that same single mom can, and will, rise when given the opportunity. The focus of every program to help the poor and the needy should be centered on making poverty temporary, not just tolerable.

It has also become clear that America must continue to rise as the leader of the free world. It doesn't mean that we play policeman for the world or fight endless wars. My travels to other countries as a member of Congress showed me that when America shrinks and withdraws from the world stage, tyrants always step up, despair sets in, and freedom begins to falter. America must rise to stand with our allies and freedom-loving people everywhere; it is who we are, and it is what we must do.

I believe the American people, and freedom-loving people everywhere, deserve the opportunity to rise to the occasion! But honestly, this isn't about Washington. It's about us. It's about you and me and what we are willing to do.

The coming years are going to determine whether

Benjamin Franklin was right—that our nation really is a rising sun. I simply refuse to believe America's best days are behind us and that we are doomed on the downward path of the setting sun.

I am convinced that as long as we get government out of our way and give our citizens the opportunity to rise, we will experience the power of what Ronald Reagan became famous for repeating—it is "Morning in America." I believe it is still morning in America; we just need to transcend the political divisiveness to greet the dawn.

Your political beliefs do not have to be tied to a specific candidate. It's about the policies, not the politicians. The people of this country still have a voice and must advocate for principles and policies. I learned how to use my voice as an elected official, and now I have opportunity to raise my voice, lead with character, and impact others from a different point on the compass.

Journeying from the structured world of the United States Capitol to the televised world of CNN was an interesting adjustment, to say the least. I had to quickly transition into becoming a political commentator. I was happy to be able to offer an unleashed and unrestricted perspective, now that I was released from the bonds of being a dutiful politician where I was forever being herded by the party, politicians, lobbyists, and consultants. I love the added freedom and confidence it gives me to raise my voice on the principles I care the most about.

Earlier in this book I shared how leadership of both parties strives to keep members off balance and busy, distracted and dependent. This is what leads to the bigger problem in Washington these days—collusion. We often complain about conflict between the parties, but the bigger issue is actually how the leaders of both parties collude to avoid difficult votes or to pass out-of-control spending packages. I remind people often that it is impossible to get $30 trillion in debt through conflict—you can rack up that much debt only by colluding/agreeing to spending together.

I am still a Republican, and I am still strong. Although I no longer hold an official office position, I am engaged in the political scene and continue to share my views on matters that are important to me and to the American people.

Looking to the future of the White House and Congress, it's troubling to see such drastic and distinct polarization, where people are more willing to back politicians than policies without even taking the time to review their platforms. There is little to no leverage or compromise available, especially as cancel culture continues to devour any chance for real, elevated discussion.

Inside a party, you can be canceled by party purity tests. Often when you compromise, to the purists it means you are a squish and a sellout and that you will likely face a primary challenger in your next election. The other end is when you question anything you aren't just disagreeing, but you are perceived as attacking someone's truth and you should be run out of town. Neither leads to better conversation.

I believe that as members of the conservative party, we have failed to bring our message to and connect with women and racial minorities. For this reason, our nation has suffered. This critical failure has allowed our opponents to define and manipulate the Republican Party's principles, as a whole.

The future success of the Republican Party will be determined by its ability to extend the invitation to diverse perspectives and voices, instead of simply tolerating them. Our policy solutions must be personal, not transactional. There are not Democratic issues and Republican issues—only American issues.

If you really stop and think about what matters to most Americans, you will discover that most Americans are worried about the same issues and believe in the same basic principles to solve those issues.

America is the only country in history that isn't based on geography or common heritage. America is based on principles, an ideal, and an idea. I believe that people and principles are more important that political parties and politicians.

CHAPTER 13

Qualified Women

No one is really sure who said it first, but whoever said it, said it best, "Empowered women empower women." Short, simple, and powerful. I believe it because I have been blessed by it. My goal has always been to live my life in such a way that I can empower others the way I have been empowered by amazing women.

I have shared in this book the story of my amazing mother. She empowered me. She continues to empower me—and not just by her hard work, sacrifice, and example over a lifetime. She empowered me because she trusted me from a very early age. She trusted that I could accept big challenges and rise to them.

When I was in school, she trusted that I would get my homework done before I went on to other activities. She trusted that I could handle myself properly on color guard trips or late-night drama rehearsals. She believed I would treat others with respect and dignity—no matter what.

Some may say that my mom had to trust me because of her grueling work schedule. While necessity may have been important, that isn't how trust works. Even when trust is mission-critical, it cannot be asked for, demanded, or even bestowed. Trust is a natural by-product of living up to your principles and demonstrating trustworthiness.

Most of the time my mom didn't even need to use words. The look on her face conveyed a quiet confidence that validated me to my core when I did things right. She also had a look for when she thought I could do better or when I hadn't lived up to the best that was in me.

Honest, genuine, authentic trust may well be the most empowering thing on the planet. I have tried to apply this to my children and to so many women, especially the young women I worked with while in office. "I trust you! You got this! Make it happen!" were all expressions I used frequently as I tried to empower and elevate women in the workplace, at home, and in the public square.

Because of my mother, I never used the political expression so often deployed by politicians: "Trust me."

In fact, when I would talk to constituents I would say, "I will not ask you to trust me. Just watch me."

My mom worked really hard and simply didn't have time to go to many of my competitions and performances. Joyce Neffrage, who was my friend Lisa's mom, became the mom for several of us on color guard. She truly was like a mom to me. More than cheering me on in competitions, more than the many times she fed me or drove me from an event, more than the accumulated time she waited for me to come out of my house while she waited in the car—Joyce taught me the powerful principle of positive expectations.

Joyce would always say to me, "Mia, one day I'm gonna see your name in lights. Maybe it will be on Broadway, and maybe it will be somewhere else. I just know you are going to make it big!

"You're too good to keep to yourself," she would say. "I know you are going to accomplish big and important things one day."

It amazed me that somebody who was not my own mom would tell me such things. As far as I was concerned, I was the only one she was saying such things to, and I even wondered if she was saying such things to her own daughter. Of course, later I would realize that she did this for so many—because Joyce was an empowered woman and knew how to empower young women.

I have had many wonderful female friends who have

empowered me in so many ways. One friend who was one of the few people I knew from junior high to high school to college to today is Becky Rosenbluth. Even though she was a year ahead of me in school, we developed a great friendship. Becky empowered me through her commitment to excellence and her deep compassion.

Becky was like a big sister to me. We did all our music stuff together. She had an amazing voice. It was a voice of steel. There wasn't a note that that girl couldn't hit. Becky was all about achieving excellence. She taught me to recognize the price of success, and then she inspired me to be willing to pay that price. Becky demonstrated the importance of achieving alongside others rather than over others. She knew that both of us could pursue and achieve excellence together—complementing rather than competing, encouraging rather than undermining, lifting rather than belittling.

After Becky graduated from high school she went to the Hartt School of Music. I admit that after she left for school, I felt a little lost and alone for a while. Then I got to visit her on campus. She showed me what it took to excel in music on a college campus. But she didn't stop there. She told me I had what it took to join her and other talented people in the school of music. Becky told me to get ready, audition, and prepare to join her the following fall. With that empowerment, I auditioned and ended up getting a half scholarship for music.

Some people are great on their own but are not great team players or coaches. It is the difference between being a great individual player—like in golf, tennis, or cross-country—and being the point guard on the basketball team who can not only excel individually but makes everyone else on the team better.

Becky was always really compassionate. I remember in school when we would have an open period and get into her big car and find as much loose change as we could. For some crazy reason, she always had money just laying around in the car. Sometimes, on some of those days where my funds were low and I needed a little midday break, that loose change was like manna from heaven. I am not sure if Becky would just toss it around whenever she got paid or if she purposefully put it there so I could find it on those days.

Once we found enough change, we would drive over to Bagel King. Becky would get the exact same thing every time—a salted bagel, toasted with cream cheese. I would get a plain bagel, toasted with cream cheese. As wonderful as it was to have a good bagel, it was more important to have good conversation with a good friend.

Becky is a most extraordinary example of empowering others through her example of excellence combined with immense compassion. Becky really is what leadership in our communities, businesses, and government should look like. She made me better, she inspired me to want to be better, and she helped me learn how to empower others to become better.

I have mentioned the empowering impact of my Yacht Club sisters. They have strengthened, uplifted, and empowered me in more ways than I can count. There is one lesson they taught me that we don't talk about often enough: They have shown me how courageous vulnerability is vital to being strong and strengthening others.

Social media and societal norms often suggest, in not-so-subtle ways, that perfection is what you must outwardly project and inwardly achieve. The message is clear: Every Instagram story and Facebook post must portray an image of pure awesomeness. If you do not have it all together and cannot properly frame it up in that selfie or snap that picture of your gourmet meal and share a moment from your amazing vacation, you are somehow less than. Sadly, these pictures of perfection are not only not real, but they also prevent us from being and becoming our most powerful, authentic, and influential selves.

Hiding behind the masks of perfection in our schools and churches, at work or with friends, may seem like what we are supposed to do, but it is wreaking havoc on our psychological well-being and sinking our souls.

There are so many women today who deal with overwhelming anxiety, deep depression, and despair. I have learned to love the term "courageous vulnerability" as a way to celebrate scar tissue and find the beauty and power in our brokenness. If there is one motto of the Yacht Club, it is "Keeping it real." I hadn't realized that keeping it real actually takes real courage.

Breaking down the facade of perfection and fixing the underlying anxiety starts with honest, authentic conversations in our homes and communities. During our lunches or dinners together, the Yacht Club has dealt with issues of cancer, death, fear, frustration, work, kids, spouses, bosses, success, failure, and everything in between. And of course, courageous vulnerability also empowers you to tell your friends that they have spinach in their teeth, are experiencing a wardrobe malfunction or fashion faux pas, or are about to make a really bad dessert decision or unwise life choice.

I have come to believe that courageous vulnerability may be one of the most important leadership attributes for the twenty-first century. Leaders who show courageous vulnerability create an empowering space for others to do the same.

Author Brené Brown wrote, "Vulnerability sounds like truth and feels like courage. Truth and courage aren't always comfortable, but they're never weakness."[1]

Empowered women empowering women begins with young women. We need to have different conversations with our girls and prepare them for the challenges ahead. I love what Senator Ben Sasse, a Republican from Nebraska, wrote in his book *The Vanishing American*

Adult, about how we are often bubble-wrapping our kids in an attempt to protect them from failure, discomfort, or pain. The message sent is that failure is fatal, and teens should never risk looking bad in front of others. Senator Sasse believes we should do the opposite. He says we should celebrate "scar tissue."[2] Falling off of a bike, failing to make the softball team, losing a class election, or being rejected for a job are all opportunities for growth and may contain critical life lessons. Following the old adage of seeing failure as fertilizer for future success might be exactly the message our young women need.

The women of the Congressional Black Caucus demonstrated to me that empowered women are comfortable with differences and long for depth. For women in Congress, it is still an uphill battle. Learning to value the differences makes all the difference. Everyone can learn something from anyone if you are empowered and confident enough to listen.

Representative Martha Roby, a Republican from Alabama, empowered me by embracing her story and teaching me to exhale. Martha was the first member of Congress I knew who fully embraced talking about and leaning into the need to have the voices of mothers in our nation's capital. She would often say, "No one can fill the void of a mother's voice in this institution." Mothers have always been the voice for the children of the nation.

Martha was unapologetically a mom first. Her voice was vital in ensuring the children of America were watched over and cared for in Congress. She helped me see the power and importance of my "mom voice."

Representative Roby also helped me learn the art of the exhale, which in and of itself is empowering. So many today feel like they have to have instant certainty on every developing news story and a hot take for every rumor echoing down the marbled halls of the Capitol. Sadly, many members of Congress buy into the need for a hot take filled with anger, rage, and contempt for those who dare to disagree with them.

Not long after President Trump had uttered his expletive-laced and denigrating statement about the people of Haiti, I was sitting in the Republican Party Conference meeting in Washington. During the course of the meeting, the topic of immigration came up. Representative Glenn Grothman stood and actually defended the president's comments. And not only did he defend them, but he also extended the arrogant, egotistical, and uneducated sentiments about a people I call family and a place my parents once called home.

As I listened, my heart started racing and my blood began to boil. I was getting ready to unleash the mother of all hot takes. Martha Roby was sitting next to me. She softly said, "Mia, we are just going to let the rage fade. Just exhale and sit with it for a minute." I exhaled and sat. Martha asked, "You okay?" I exhaled again. As I exhaled, a very calm, clear, and direct idea came to me.

I looked over at the leadership members, who were all still sitting and listening to Representative Grothman. During a pause, I asked the leadership, "Are you okay with this?" I calmly continued, "He clearly sees the people of Haiti as inferior. Do you see me as inferior? If you do not see me as an equal, you can remove me from this conference. If we don't see everyone as equal under God, we have bigger problems."

In an instant, the members of the conference stood in support. The leadership members followed and also stood. We were standing together for an important, fundamental principle that everyone was created equal. With the entire conference standing, I simply said that it was now time for Representative Grothman to sit down.

Martha empowered me that day in a way that I will never forget.

Representative Marcia Fudge, my Democratic friend, also empowered me by having my best interest in mind, even when it wasn't hers. Messaging bills are used by both political parties to score points and serve as ammunition for elections. Democrat and Republican leaders love to force hard votes on tough issues. Marcia protected me from messaging bills. Such bills are simply what the name describes—a message for constituents. Messaging bills aren't designed to pass or become law.

The bills are designed to be hard to vote against. For example, a bill could be called the "We Shall Have Clean Air" bill but be filled with a host of awful policies about taxes and health care. It becomes a problem when the hometown news outlet carries a headline, "Congressman Votes Against Clean Air." Messaging bills are great for fund-raising or to create wedge issues for campaign commercials. But they waste priceless time and attention in Congress. When such a bill would come to the floor, Marcia would sometimes come to me and suggest, "Don't vote for this—it isn't good for you."

Messaging bills rarely pass, but they do wreak havoc on members. It represents the worst of politics. Marcia would have my back with members of the CBC when I voted differently, especially on messaging bills. I felt empowered because I knew Marcia loved me enough to tell me to do something that was in my best interest that wasn't really in hers. She loved me and still loves me; she is an empowered woman.

Representative Cathy McMorris Rodgers, a Republican from Washington, was the woman who encouraged me more than any to raise my voice and use it. She challenged me to communicate more. Even though we were from the same political party, many members play this zero-sum game of who will get on the cable news shows and who will get published in major news outlets. Cathy has an abundance mentality and knows what being willing to raise your voice—especially as a female member of Congress—can mean.

Cathy was also one of those fierce mothers in the House. She has a son with Down syndrome. She had learned the communication nuances of eyes, smiles, and countenance, and the extraordinary way our Down syndrome friends communicate in ways the rest of us can't.

Cathy taught me that we stand taller and stronger as a society when we stand with those who cannot stand for themselves. Our Down syndrome friends are fellow travelers with us along the road of life. While they may struggle with some of the daily tasks the rest of us take for granted, they possess skills and abilities we all would be wise to emulate. They may struggle with speech, but their capacity to love is endless and doesn't require them to utter a word. They may have difficulty making decisions, but they never judge and have an amazing ability to accept everyone for who they are. They may strain to work or learn, yet they seem to be forever teaching us about where simple joy is to be found and what it means to discover and cherish true happiness.

Cathy empowered me to raise my voice, use my voice, and deploy my voice for all, especially for those who can't raise their own.

As a woman walking into crowded rooms of men, it would have been easy for me to turn around and walk right back out. It can be intimidating to have the only different viewpoint and terrifying to stand up on the podium and boldly ask others to look at things in a different way—a way they may not be used to.

Not only do I ask for women to lift up other women, but I ask for men to also help empower women. Empowering women as a man shows that you are secure enough in your masculinity to encourage women rather than disparaging them. I tell my children when they are looking for someone to marry, "You are not looking for a spouse; you are looking for a partner." I say this because my husband has been a partner to me. He does not see me as inferior. When we were attending an event once, someone asked him, "How did you let your wife into politics?" And he responded, "Can you imagine trying to contain lightning in a glass bottle?"

He recognized and called out what I had in me. I had gifts and talents that could be used for the betterment of society, and he didn't see my career in politics as threatening. He saw us as partners going on this adventure together—not for the benefit of ourselves, but for the benefit of society.

There are women who have special gifts and talents, and they're meant for the betterment of society. I often shared with my girls a sentiment attributed to Brigham Young that speaks to female capability and how if we were to walk into the areas predominantly run by men, we would "enlarge [our] sphere of usefulness for the benefit of society at large."[3] This is why one of my daughters is studying aerospace engineering; she knew she had certain gifts and talents, and she went beyond asking about normal occupations for women and entered into STEM, where there were few women. Somehow society has taught us to believe that men are better at these things, and we don't even stop to question it.

I am proud for my children to see that their mom was elected to government positions and see that all the other goals are not unreachable, but very possible. A lot of times we believe we can do it because we see someone else we relate to do it. Sometimes it takes that image. One day another young girl will see my daughter be the first woman to build a rocket to land the first person on Mars and want to pursue aerospace engineering too.

Every single woman should be looking at ways she can get involved, not for herself, but to enlarge the sphere of knowledge and to make sure that other girls see that they can do these things too. If we continue to do this, our society will become completely different. In the next generation, the more women get involved, the more you're going to see women do magnificent things. This is not just about our own confidence; it's about the competence of the future.

Empowered women empowering other women will echo down through the ages. It will shape the future. For me it is about a young girl, maybe even my granddaughter or great-granddaughter, saying, "Yes, I can run for Congress, soar to the heavens, make a difference in my community, be an extraordinary mom, run a business, and be a difference maker."

Trust, positive words, excellence, compassion, courageous vulnerability, depth, and looking out for one another's interest are all crucial in helping qualified women feel qualified and be qualified. I am most thankful for *all* the empowered women who have empowered me over my life and career.

CHAPTER 14

Unfinished

We live in a country full of opportunity, but it is up to you to take advantage of that opportunity. It's time to take advantage of the liberties, freedoms, and chances we've been so blessed to have.

No matter what arena you find yourself in, no matter what your background or résumé says, no matter what opposition comes your way, your story has value, and I want to empower you to be bold enough to share it.

Your history, story, and beliefs qualify your words. Say something. Use your voice. Be confident. Move to action. Get involved. Don't be afraid to fail. If you fail, start again.

A particular note to those in the minority community:

Whether you are Black, a woman, or a Black woman, you have the opportunity today to share your story, raise your voice, lead with character, and empower others. What you believe and what matters to you—matters! Your diversity and minority qualities are a benefit that the majority is without. You bring a unique and valuable view to the table; you can speak for those who have no voice and can also speak for the good of all. It is critical for you to recognize that your community and our country don't need you to speak out only on minority issues; the country needs you to speak out on every issue. We will need your unique perspective if we are going to solve problems and overcome challenges.

It is vital for each American to recognize that leading doesn't come without struggles, doubt, and hardship. There are times when you may question yourself or times when others will question you, but it is then that you can rely on the strength of your story and the content of your character in order to have the confidence to take action and speak up. Learn from your mistakes, put your head down, and get to work.

As I experienced two congressional race losses, I also achieved some things that will go down in the history of the United States of America. Although I faced opposition, doubt, and questions, I found a way to persevere to fulfill my duty and my purpose and proudly represent the people. Whether in an elected position or lobbying for policies outside a formal office, I found power in my story and cannot help but share it.

The United States of America needs your voice and needs to hear your story. You are qualified. Find your voice, lead with character, and empower others to do the same. America needs you, and the nation is waiting for your influence to make it a more perfect union.

In January 2021, I watched the inauguration of Joseph Biden as the forty-sixth president of the United States of America. President Biden wasn't my choice to lead the country; neither was his predecessor. But I watched that most amazing moment of the transfer of power from one administration to the next. While the process was more turbulent and troublesome than most in our history, I took courage and confidence that the republic stood strong, the Constitution held, the institutions of government endured, and the business of "we the people" marched on.

I watched the poet and self-described "skinny black girl" Amanda Gorman as she stood before the world, qualified by the content of her character, and provided a moment that was as inspired as it was inspiring. Amanda Gorman owned her story; she had found her voice and was raising it in a most extraordinary way. I saw in her something of my younger self.

She obviously had never been on such a stage before, and I could sense early on that she might have been questioning herself and whether or not she belonged on such a stage at such a moment. She quickly settled that in her mind and gained confidence as she dynamically and powerfully conveyed her message:

> When day comes we ask ourselves,
> where can we find light in this
> never-ending shade?
> The loss we carry,
> a sea we must wade.
> We've braved the belly of the beast,
> We've learned that quiet isn't always peace,
> and the norms and notions
> of what just is
> isn't always just-ice.
> And yet the dawn is ours
> before we knew it.
> Somehow we do it.
> Somehow we've weathered and witnessed
> a nation that isn't broken,
> but simply unfinished.[1]

Amanda Gorman's words, "a nation that isn't broken, but simply unfinished," reverberated in my soul. I found myself back on my swearing-in day, running with my "all in, all the time" husband Jason, on the "unfinished" and "under-construction" National Mall.

As Jason and I stood before Lincoln, we could hear the echo of Dr. King's words across the mall. I could sense in a significant way that, like our nation's capital, our character is always under construction.

In the midst of the Civil War, leaders from around the world—and even citizens on both sides of the conflict here at home—wondered if the grand American experiment in democracy was doomed to decline. Many mused, quite loudly, that it appeared that the Civil War was the beginning of the end of the United States of America.

With the battle between North and South raging on, resources were scarce, human suffering surged, and uncertainty about the future of the Union enveloped the minds of the people. Washington, DC, was weak and under constant threat. The unfinished dome of the Capitol Building served as a visual reminder of the precarious position of the nation and the uncertain future of American democracy.

Abraham Lincoln was determined to preserve the Union by any and every possible means. In a show of pure confidence in his belief in what the future held for the nation, Lincoln ensured that the work on the Capitol continued without pause. The rising Capitol dome was a bold, audacious, and powerful declaration—and a visual punctuation—that America would stand united for generations to come.

Above all, Lincoln was putting to rest the notion that

the Civil War was the beginning of the end. Instead, he wanted the people and the world to know that the current conflict was merely the end of the beginning of the onward march of freedom.

Lincoln's character and his plan, found within the parentheses of a crazy idea, would lay the groundwork for Dr. King and countless others—including my parents and me—to have a place in the world to build the content of our character and prove we were qualified to pursue our own crazy ideas within the parentheses of America.

Standing in that completed Capitol dome as a member of Congress was a humbling and empowering experience that never got old.

Now, one of the things I learned running around the halls of the United States Congress is that the depiction in Aaron Sorkin's classic television show *The West Wing* isn't really what happens on most days in DC. But *West Wing* moments did happen from time to time. And, interestingly, most of those moments were connected not to politics but to people of character.

One of the most powerful scenes from *The West Wing* occurred in an episode when the president's chief of staff, Leo McGarry, a recovering alcoholic, reached out to a struggling staffer, Josh Lyman. When Lyman asked the often-surly McGarry why he had waited hours for him to come out of a counseling session, McGarry responded with a story:

This guy is walking down a street when he falls in a hole. The walls are so steep he can't get out. A doctor passes by and the guy shouts up, "Hey you, can you help me out?" The doctor writes a prescription, throws it down in the hole, and moves on. Then a priest comes along and the guy shouts up, "Father, I'm down in this hole, can you help me out?" The priest writes out a prayer, throws it down in the hole, and moves on. Finally, a friend walks by. "Hey Joe, it's me, can you help me out?" And the friend jumps in the hole! Our guy says, "Are you stupid? Now we're both down here." The friend says, "Yeah, but I've been down here before...And I know the way out!"[2]

I am a Black Republican woman who served in the House of Representatives for four years, as well as various other political positions. I created policies and advocated for change for the benefit of the underdogs and underrepresented groups. I have been down into the bottom of that deep hole where the feelings of uncertainty, being unqualified, and unprepared foster real fear. I get it. I am ready to jump into the hole with you. I am far from perfect, and I continue to learn what it means to be qualified and how to develop the content of my character. What I have learned, however, is that I do know the way out and the way up.

Our nation has also been down in the depths of that big black hole. Often, we landed there because we failed to live up to the principles we profess to believe.

Gettysburg has a special place in my heart. It obviously holds deep meaning for America and American citizens—especially those whose ancestors were slaves. Lincoln was often derided for his gangly looks, his high-pitched voice, his humble beginnings. If anyone could have questioned whether or not he was qualified, it was Lincoln. The content of his character qualified him.

In a speech to honor the fallen dead, Lincoln concluded with a clarion call for the living. The final section of the Gettysburg Address challenges us to gratefully remember those who gave their all, lifts our gaze toward the great task and test before us as a nation, and implores us to be *highly resolved* in our commitment to the future of freedom.

Consider Lincoln's final call and question:

> It is for us the living, rather, to be dedicated here to the unfinished work which they who fought here have thus far so nobly advanced. It is rather for us to be here dedicated to the great task remaining before us—that from these honored dead we take increased devotion to that cause for which they gave the last full measure of devotion—that we here *highly resolve* that these dead shall not have died in vain—that this nation, under God, shall have a new

birth of freedom, and that government of the people, by the people, for the people, shall not perish from the earth.[3] [Emphasis added.]

Will we be dedicated to the unfinished work and the task before us? Will we take increased devotion to the cause? Will we be highly resolved to a new birth of freedom in our time? These are the questions Lincoln still asks of each of us today. Lincoln was and is challenging us to be qualified by the content of our character and live determined lives so that we can make a difference.

Our nation's capital will always be unfinished—as will be you, me, and the rest of America. We all need to remember to take confidence that we aren't broken, just unfinished.

When it comes to politics, the past few years have caused many to question whether or not the Republican Party is redeemable, salvageable, or if it has simply been broken beyond repair. Detractors pin the future prospects of the party to a personality and politician who took the GOP through the past seven years. I think the party, like the country, is simply unfinished. I said then, and I reiterate now, that the principles are the thing that matter most.

I know conservative principles work because I have seen them work—as a mother, as a mayor, and as a member of

Congress. The GOP should continue to be the conservator and champion of those principles. If the party is going to move beyond the battles of 2016, 2020, and 2022, we must return to the principles that transform lives and communities while sustaining freedom for our country.

In 1964 Ronald Reagan delivered to a television audience a speech that became known as "A Time for Choosing." I think Reagan got it right when he declared, "You and I are told increasingly we have to choose between a left or right. Well I'd like to suggest there is no such thing as a left or right. There's only an up or down—[up] man's old-aged dream, the ultimate in individual freedom consistent with law and order, or down to the ant heap of totalitarianism."[4]

Republicans shouldn't spend a minute talking about the past fights, past personalities, and the previous president's backward-facing grievance message. Fighting the last war is never a winning strategy.

I have stated numerous times as a member of Congress and as a media commentator on CNN that campaigns are never about what was, or even what is, but are always about what's next.

If conservatives want to reclaim the confidence of a large swath of the American people, they must reconnect voters to principles that can be pegged to solutions for pressing problems.

I actually agree with Hillary Clinton that "it takes a

village." I just happen to believe that the village is the village, the community, and the family—not the government.

Conservatives have to make the case of what they are for, not just what they are against. Being against big government, taxes, and regulation is important. More important is connecting the dots for people to see that what we are for are the principles and policies that will empower citizens to live their own version of the American Dream.

Making the case for conservatism should begin in minority communities, which are very community connected, family centered, and entrepreneurially engaged. Minority communities should be invited not to just join the party but to lead the movement.

If the Republican Party chooses to focus forward, it can transcend the divisiveness of the past seven years and show that the party is not broken, just unfinished. I promise that wherever I am, and whatever opportunities arise, I will raise my voice in the promotion of conservative principles and policies while never again allowing personalities, consumed with their own power, to drive the party.

———————

There are many things that I miss about running around Washington as a member of Congress. Some are big and important; others are small and seemingly insignificant.

I miss the people—my colleagues from both sides of the aisle who were patient with me, taught me, challenged me, and empowered me. I miss the daily interaction with a group of committed staff members who worked around the clock to serve the people, do the work, and contribute to the work of the people. Constituents' visits were my favorite—an opportunity to listen and learn and then to be able to share the "People's House" and the principles of freedom with them. I miss the sound of high heels clicking quickly down the marbled halls. It meant there was a woman in a hurry to do her job, cast a vote, chair a committee, or raise her voice on an issue.

It was a distinct privilege to simply walk through sacred spaces in the Capitol. I miss that. I can't begin to describe the number of times I would just stop and soak in the feeling of the building. At times it was overwhelming to me. I felt a deep connection to the others who have held office and walked the halls. I especially loved all the symbolism found in the Capitol. Every statue, painting, ceiling, and door held images that ultimately connected to principles of freedom, faith, and the future promise of America.

Yes, I do miss my morning runs on the National Mall! It was my time with the magic of the morning sun, the monuments, and the thoughts inspired from the cradle of freedom. Running was where I could put all the puzzle pieces together of what it meant to be qualified and what to do with what I had learned. Every run was a master class for me in my own unfinished development as a leader, a mom, a citizen, and an individual.

The first run Jason and I took on the morning before I was sworn in as a member of Congress was also the lesson for everything I needed to remember before leaving office and beginning a new season of life.

On that first run, after Jason and I finished pausing to look out across the under-construction and unfinished National Mall from the steps of the Lincoln Memorial, we each took a deep breath. We looked at each other, gathered our combined courage, and said to each other, "Let's run!"

We continue to run. To paraphrase Robert Frost, there are promises *for us* to keep and miles to go before *we* sleep.[5] Exciting opportunities and significant challenges are ahead. New ways to lead, serve, and make a difference abound for us—*and for you!*

Run with me! Lead and lift others! *Win!*

My goal, as we continue to run together, is for you to redefine your definition of "qualified." My hope is that by putting the content of your character first, you will create a future of freedom, opportunity, and qualified success that will last.

You are qualified! You have a voice! You can lead with character! You can empower others!

So, let's run!

Acknowledgments

There are simply too many individuals to acknowledge in this book who have made a difference for me on this journey. Family, friends, constituents, colleagues, and extraordinary staff have all contributed in ways too big to describe and in critical moments too many to count. You all know who you are, and I hope you had some moments in this book that made you smile and gave you a second to reflect on what *we* accomplished together along with the difference you have made in the process.

I also know there is an innumerable army of supporters I have never met who have a seat of honor at my table. Many of these amazing souls simply let me know they were praying for me. Some made great sacrifices just to make an individual contribution because they believed in the cause. Others voluntarily spent countless hours organizing events, hanging signs, making calls, knocking on doors, serving constituents, waiting for me to come out of a meeting, and so much more.

You proved to me that one person can make a difference. *Each* of you made a difference for me. I hope you see your efforts reflected in these pages. I pray you will sense my gratitude for your service and sacrifice.

Notes

Introduction

1 https://www.archives.gov/files/social-media/transcripts/transcript
-march-pt3-of-3-2602934.pdf.
2 Boyd C. Matheson, "America Lives Within the Parentheses of a
Crazy Idea," *Deseret News*, September 12, 2019, https://www
.deseret.com/2019/9/12/20862450/america-lives-within-the
-parentheses-of-a-crazy-idea-9-11-pentagon-trump-melania.
3 Soo Youn, "Women Are Less Aggressive Than Men When Applying
for Jobs, Despite Getting Hired More Frequently: LinkedIn," ABC
News, March 7, 2019, https://abcnews.go.com/Business/women
-aggressive-men-applying-jobs-hired-frequently-linkedin/story?id
=61531741.

1. Do I Belong in a Sea of Old White Men?

1 *Sesame Street*, "One of These Things (Is Not Like the Others),"
SongLyrics, http://www.songlyrics.com/sesame-street/one-of-these
-things-is-not-like-the-others-lyrics/.

2. Owning Your Story

1 Boyd Matheson, "Insight over Incite: Protests Should Spark
Uncomfortable—and Elevated—Conversations," *Deseret News*,
June 4, 2020, https://www.deseret.com/opinion/2020/6/4/21279828
/george-floyd-protests-civil-unrest-insight-incite-cruicial-conversations.

3. You Have a Voice—Raise It!

1 https://theimaginativeconservative.org/2011/08/quote-of-day
-mans-finest-hour.html.

4. Hinges the Size of Midges

1   Boyd Matheson, "Power Couples: 4 Inspiring Political Relationships and What to Learn from Them, KSL-TV Studio Five, February 11, 2022, https://studio5.ksl.com/power-couples-4-inspiring-political -relationships/.

5. Running to, Not Away

1   Associated Press, "Final Total of Mayor Bloomberg's 2009 Campaign: $109M," silive.com, July 15, 2010, https://www .silive.com/news/2010/07/final_total_of_mayor_bloomberg.html.
2   Oliver Burkeman, "Why Feeling Like a Fraud Can Be a Good Thing," BBC News, April 25, 2016, https://www.bbc.com/news /magazine-36082469.
3   David Goodfriend, "Justice Sonia Sotomayor Explains Class in the U.S. Better Than Anyone," *HuffPost*, February 26, 2013, https: //www.huffpost.com/entry/justice-sonya-sotomayor-e_b_2760715.
4   Amela Trokic, "Imposter Syndrome: The Story of the Involuntary Swindler," Atlantbh, November 15, 2017, https://www.atlantbh.com /imposter-syndrome-story-involuntary-fraud/.
5   Tavi Gevinson, "I Want It to Be Worth It: An Interview with Emma Watson," *Rookie*, May 27, 2013, https://www.rookiemag.com/2013 /05/emma-watson-interview/2/.
6   Dr. Valerie Young, "The 5 Types of Impostors," Impostor Syndrome Institute, https://impostorsyndrome.com/articles/5-types-of -impostors/.

6. Bounce-ability and Making History

1   Porter B. Williamson, *Gen. Patton's Principles for Life and Leadership* (Tucson: Management and Systems Consultants, 1988), p. 1.

7. Qualified for "Good Trouble"

1   Robert F. Kennedy, "Statement on Assassination of Martin Luther King, Jr., Indianapolis, Indiana, April 4, 1968," John F. Kennedy

Presidential Library and Museum, https://www.jfklibrary.org/learn
/about-jfk/the-kennedy-family/robert-f-kennedy/robert-f-kennedy
-speeches/statement-on-assassination-of-martin-luther-king-jr
-indianapolis-indiana-april-4-1968.

2 "Welfare Square," Church of Jesus Christ of Latter-day Saints
(website), https://www.churchofjesuschrist.org/learn/welfare-square.

8. "So You're Telling Me There's a Chance"

1 "Jackie Robinson: This I Believe," NPR, March 25, 2008, audio,
https://www.npr.org/templates/story/story.php?storyId=89030535.

2 Quoted in Donna Brazile, "A People's Struggle," *Daily Herald*
(Columbia, TN), August 4, 2013, https://www.columbiadailyherald
.com/story/opinion/columns/2013/08/04/a-people-s-struggle
/25653176007/.

3 Glenn Kessler, "Tim Scott Often Talks About His Grandfather and
Cotton. There's More to That Tale," *Washington Post*, April 23,
2021, https://www.washingtonpost.com/politics/2021/04/23/tim
-scott-often-talks-about-his-grandfather-cotton-theres-more-tale/.

4 Michele L. Norris, "Judge Jackson's Long Journey to the Court—and
Ours," *Washington Post*, April 9, 2022, https://www.washingtonpost
.com/opinions/2022/04/09/justice-jackson-racism-supreme-court/.

9. Declaring Your Character in an Age of Reputation

1 Andrew Hill with John Wooden, *Be Quick—But Don't Hurry!* (New
York: Simon & Schuster, 2001).

2 David Badash, "Joe Manchin: 'This Job's Not Worth It to Me to Sell
My Soul,'" *Raw Story*, May 29, 2021, https://www.rawstory.com
/joe-manchin-this-jobs-not-worth-it-to-me-to-sell-my-soul/.

3 William George Jordan, *The Power of Truth* (Cambridge, MA:
University Press, 1902), Project Gutenberg, https://www.gutenberg
.org/files/56020/56020-h/56020-h.htm.

4 Boyd C. Matheson, "Finding the Road to Happiness in 2018,"
Deseret News, January 1, 2018, https://www.deseret.com/2018
/1/1/20624720/boyd-matheson-finding-the-road-to-happiness-in
-2018.

Notes

11. Raising Dreamers and Leading Others

1   David Brooks, "Seeing Each Other Deeply," *Y Magazine*, Winter 2020, Brigham Young University, https://magazine.byu.edu/article/seeing-each-other-deeply/.

2   Brigham Young, *Journal of Discourses*, vol. 13 (Liverpool, UK, 1871), http://www.mormonismi.net/jod/13.txt.

3   TEDx Talks, "The Myth of Average: Todd Rose at TEDxSonomaCounty," YouTube, June 19, 2013, video, https://www.youtube.com/watch?v=4eBmyttcfU4.

4   M. L. Stedman, *The Light Between Oceans* (New York: Scribner, 2012).

12. The Future of Principles over Politics

1   John Wagner, "Mia Love Gives Trump No Love as She Concedes a Narrow Loss in Utah," *Washington Post*, November 26, 2018, https://www.washingtonpost.com/politics/mia-love-gives-trump-no-love-as-she-concedes-a-narrow-loss-in-utah/2018/11/26/2062c158-f1a5-11e8-80d0-f7e1948d55f4_story.html.

2   "The Rising Sun Armchair (George Washington's Chair)," USHistory.org, https://www.ushistory.org/more/sun.htm.

13. Qualified Women

1   Natalie Snyder, "*Daring Greatly: How the Courage to Be Vulnerable Transforms the Way We Live, Love, Parent, and Lead* by Brene Brown. Salty Souls Experience," Salty Souls, September 5, 2016, https://saltysoulsexperience.com/daring-greatly-brene-brown/.

2   "Interview with Sen. Ben Sasse," *New Day*, CNN, May 16, 2017, transcript, http://www.cnn.com/TRANSCRIPTS/1705/16/nday.06.html.

3   Brigham Young, *Journal of Discourses*, vol. 13 (Liverpool, UK, 1871), http://www.mormonismi.net/jod/13.txt.

14. Unfinished

1   "READ: Transcript of Amanda Gorman's Inaugural Poem," *Hill*, January 20, 2021, https://thehill.com/homenews/news/535052-read-transcript-of-amanda-gormans-inaugural-poem/.

Notes

2 *The West Wing*, "Noel," teleplay by Aaron Sorkin, story by
   Peter Parnell, transcript, West Wing Transcripts, http://www
   .westwingtranscripts.com/search.php?flag=getTranscript&id=32.
3 President Lincoln delivered the 272-word Gettysburg Address on
   November 19, 1863, on the battlefield near Gettysburg, Pennsylvania.
   This copy is in the possession of Cornell University. https://rmc
   .library.cornell.edu/gettysburg/good_cause/transcript.htm.
4 Ronald Reagan, "A Time for Choosing Speech, October 27, 1964,"
   Ronald Reagan Presidential Library & Museum, https://www
   .reaganlibrary.gov/reagans/ronald-reagan/time-choosing-speech
   -october-27-1964.
5 Robert Frost, "Stopping by Woods on a Snowy Evening," Literary
   Devices, https://literarydevices.net/stopping-by-woods-on-a-snowy
   -evening/.

Index

Index

Index

Index

Index

Index

Index

Index

Index

Index

Index

About the Author

MIA LOVE became the first Black Republican woman to be elected to Congress in 2014. She served as the U.S. representative for Utah's Fourth Congressional District from 2015 to 2019. While in Congress, Love supported the Republican Party's major legislative initiatives, voting for the Tax Cuts and Jobs Act of 2017 and the repeal of the Affordable Care Act, and backed the passage of the Affordable Health Care Act of 2017. Love also assisted in pushing bipartisan legislation, which eventually became law, to reform how Congress handled sexual harassment, adding a provision ensuring that taxpayers are no longer held liable for settlements paid by Congress. She served on the House Financial Services Committee, the Congressional Black Caucus, the Select Investigative Panel on Planned Parenthood, the Congressional Western Caucus, and the Climate Solutions Caucus.

Love, the daughter of Haitian immigrants, was born in New York, studied theater in Connecticut, converted to The Church of Jesus Christ of Latter-day Saints, and settled in Utah, where she launched her career in politics. Love's first involvement came at the community level when she won a seat on the Saratoga Springs city council. In 2009, she was elected mayor of Saratoga Springs, becoming the first Black woman elected mayor in the state of Utah. Love's political journey led her to speak at the 2012 Republican National Convention and see much change take place in Congress. Love is now working for CNN as a political commentator, and she is still determined to use her voice and push for Republican policy.